PRAISE FOR *W.I.T.C.H.*

"Claire is an engaging narrator with a fascinating and unique background, which makes the book intriguing and often compelling. . . . Its defined audience [is] likely to find it fits well . . . next to books by Gabrielle Bernstein and Marianne Williamson. A well-written and thoughtful exploration of spirituality from a distinctly female perspective." —*Kirkus Reviews*

"The healing process needed on this planet to stop and unwind years of oppression and violence is just beginning. Siobhan Claire stands tall in a movement of women coming forward to facilitate and lead this conscious healing process. . . . Her story is honest and true, revealing the depths of her own struggles and how she came out the other side. Let this book hold you through your own dark night of the soul, through your healing, through your spiritual awakening and remembering of who you are." —Alexandra Roxo, bestselling author of *F*ck Like a Goddess: Heal Yourself. Reclaim Your Voice. Stand in Your Power.*

"Through unfiltered truth, resilience, and deep self-inquiry, Siobhan Claire has written a book that serves as a rally cry for women to embrace their evolution and innate power. *W.I.T.C.H.* is a beautiful invitation to get curious about everything you've been told and sink into a way of life that aligns with your agency and desires." —Richelle Fredson, book publishing coach, host of the *Bound + Determined* podcast

"I'll never forget the tingles I felt all over my body when I first heard Siobhan Claire share that *W.I.T.C.H.* stood for *Woman in Total Conscious Healing* as a participant in our Fearless Force program. It was a logical discovery and a channeled knowing at the same time! I got the feels all over again as I pored over this book. There is a W.I.T.C.H. in all of us, and Claire does an exquisite job of allowing us to tap into the fountain of magic and mystery that lies within and around us . . . with or without the pointed hat and broom." —Eduardo Placer, story doula, founder of Fearless Communicators

"New age, self-help, and alternative-health women who would receive a specific guide to refining and fine-tuning their connections with self and the spirit world will find *W.I.T.C.H.* replete with sage advice that blends metaphysical teachings with psychological discovery. . . . Its blend of autobiography, spiritual reflection, and psychic instructions creates just the right potion for readers to follow in Claire's footsteps." —Midwest Book Review

W.
I.
T.
C.
H.

W.

YOUR GUIDE

I.

TO BECOMING

T.

A WOMAN

C.

IN TOTAL

H.

CONSCIOUS HEALING

Siobhan Claire

Published by Siobhan Claire Books, New York City
www.siobhanclaire.com

Edited and designed by Girl Friday Productions
www.girlfridayproductions.com

Cover design: Megan Katsanevakis
Project management: Kristin Duran
Project editorial: Katherine Richards

ISBN (paperback): 979-8-9863943-0-5
ISBN (ebook): 979-8-9863943-1-2

Library of Congress Control Number: 2022922282

To our younger selves, who have made it this far.
To the women we are becoming.

CONTENTS

INTRODUCTION

For us women, there is no shortage of opinions about how we're supposed to be or behave, what we're supposed to believe and look like. These expectations are based on the familial, cultural, societal, and religious norms of our times, which are deeply rooted in a patriarchal way of life. We are told to be good, nice, and likable. Supportive, attentive, and selfless. Beautiful but not vain, friendly but not outspoken, smart but not too smart, sexy but not too sexy.

What?

We are conditioned to be completely disconnected from our true nature as women, to take on preapproved roles, to conform, to placate, and, in turn, to abandon ourselves. Traditional or religious stories tell us that we are supporting characters, that men lead and women follow. Our bodies, "the flesh," are described as sinful and subordinate to the mind, over which men claim dominion. The magazines of our youth sold us impossible beauty standards and products to correct our infinity of flaws. Our own mothers, who were taught by their mothers, teach us to value smallness, to take up less space, to self-restrict, to watch our weight, to be good. Our politicians work to take away bodily autonomy, to make the world less safe for us, to narrow our options. We learn to ignore our inner knowing, to dismiss any desires or needs that don't conform to patriarchal expectations. It is confusing and utterly disempowering.

The call to connect with our inner selves is always there, and some of us eventually set out on a courageous path to unlearn our conditioning and indoctrination and to redefine what it means to be a woman. What it means to be "good and worthy," to be feminine. In doing so, we experiment with embracing our bodies and our sexuality, releasing shame, integrating our shadow sides, and connecting with our intuitive gifts. This is the path of becoming Women in Total Conscious Healing. This is the path of becoming a W.I.T.C.H.

During the time of my Saturn return, after a long, difficult journey of pursuing my Olympic dream—yes, I'm talking about *the* Olympics—and then establishing my place in corporate America, I was isolated, depressed, and directionless. I had been asleep at the wheel, operating as an overachieving people pleaser and perfectionist, living an unexamined life driven by others' expectations while abandoning my own self, completely disempowered and disconnected from my body, my voice, and my desires.

Needless to say, there came a point when that was no longer working. I was guided to awaken and to take an honest look at my inner and outer realities, to remember that there is more to life and that I am worthy of love, of being seen and heard for who I am.

On my path of becoming a W.I.T.C.H., I started out by pursuing the answers to three fundamental questions:

Who am I?
What do I feel?
What do I desire?

I call this simple tool of self-discovery the conscious healing elixir.

If you are reading this book, then you're probably already

asking yourself these questions in some form or another, heeding the call to develop your intuitive gifts and define yourself from the inside out. Perhaps you are experiencing a dissonance between how you show up in the world and how you actually feel. Maybe you don't see yourself reflected in the women around you, those who have succumbed to or don't question external expectations. Maybe you are struggling to find meaning in your life or to understand what spirituality actually means to you.

The process of awakening can be confusing, lonely, tiring, and disillusioning, especially in a world that doesn't provide much space for it. Know that you are not alone. Know that it is worth it.

This is not a how-to manual for womanhood or enlightenment, and I will not preach from a pedestal but rather share my own journey of self-exploration. My hope is that this book can provide the ideas, tools, and encouragement for you to explore who you already are, to continue your unique process of awakening. Just as people do not identify as only *one* thing, there isn't *one* way to do life, and spirituality doesn't look *one* way. We are all on our own unique life path and therefore on a unique spiritual journey.

We are lucky to live in a moment when just about any creative practice is available to try: Embodiment, sensuality, song, dance, craft, cooking, gardening, acupuncture. Forest bathing, boxing, painting, drumming in a band, taking a long, hot bubble bath. That being said, we must acknowledge the fact that the practices we most often recognize as "spiritual"—the meditations, rituals, or ceremonies connected to particular cultures and religions—we have borrowed from ancient traditions. Every shiny "new" spiritual practice or teaching is rooted in the past, in our shared human history. Even the teachings we find in our Divine guidance are not new; we just awaken to remember them. Whether you take classes, read books like this one, join communities, or sit alone and create a spiritual practice based on your own inner guidance system, you are just one link in the chain. What a lovely place to be.

This leads to the question: What is spirituality? For that matter, how do I become spiritual? Do I need a guru? Do I have to dress in tie-dye and sit cross-legged on a meditation pillow in a sacred cave? Do I have to travel to a spiritual location?

Spirituality is not the domain solely of affluent white people who can afford expensive classes, yoga retreats in tropical locales, and $500 blessed candles. Nor is it the domain of some fetishized community that has somehow learned the Truth with a capital *T* by nature of their historical (and current) exploitation. Spirituality is a personal journey that does not require buckets of cash or a thousand years' worth of marginalization; it's a personal journey no matter who you are, where you're from, what you look like. Of course, feeling more at ease and in flow is simpler at a retreat, where everything is designed for that specific purpose. Nothing wrong with a little vacation every now and then. But the real magic happens in the trenches, in the mundane day-to-day, when life is neither pretty nor zen—in a fight with your significant other, at Christmas dinner with your family, while sitting in traffic, when folding the laundry, when dealing with a misogynistic client at work.

Let's explore what it means to *you* to be a woman, to be in your feminine power, and how you will live an undefined and unrestricted spiritual life, taking up space, led from a place of desire. If you are in the midst of a challenging life transition, welcome. If you are reading this book, you are already in the mindset of using this difficulty as an opportunity for reflection and growth. Maybe you're here not because life is hard at the present moment but because you've always felt a little witchy and simply want to learn more. You don't have to wait for traumatic or triggering events to start healing and rediscovering yourself. *You can start right now.*

In this book, you will learn how to identify norms, expectations, and fear-based thinking that do not belong to you; listen to your inner voice and wisdom; reconnect with your true nature; embrace the feminine; face your shadow; build a safe space; discover your coven; and build confidence in defining success for yourself and creating your own spiritual practice, your own life.

You are the creator of your life.

I'm an Olympian. I'm an Immigrant. I'm an Executive. I'm a Writer. I'm a Speaker. I'm a Singer. I'm a Coach. I'm a Spiritual Minister. I'm a Psychic Medium. I'm a Goddess. I'm a Lover. I'm a Daughter. I'm a Sister. I'm a Woman. I'm a Witch.
I'm Everything. I'm Nothing.
I'm Undefined.

Who are you?

THE GAME OF LANGUAGE: A DISCLAIMER

Throughout this book, I use language that is inescapably charged—personally, culturally, and historically. You may be averse to traditional or religious-based language, or you might be comforted by it. You might avoid patriarchal terminology of any kind, or it might not bother you so much. Language is constantly evolving, and there's no perfect way to use what can often feel like a very blunt tool. Please take care of yourself if you find that you are triggered, and though I am comfortable sparking discomfort, know that my intent is never to use words to hurt. I encourage you to rewrite in your mind with words that work for you!

God, Goddess, the Universe, Source, Spirit, the Divine, Shakti, or whatever you may call it: I encourage you to replace these terms with what feels good to you. If all of these feel off, try replacing them with *love* or *flow.*

Witch: I have chosen to reclaim this word; for me it means Woman in Total Conscious Healing. For you, *witch* could mean wise woman, *wilde* woman, healer, or, simply, woman. The choice is yours.

Pussy, vagina, vulva, yoni: For me, this is a portal to the Divine and deserves to be acknowledged and named. Many of us aren't used to addressing our most magical anatomy. I encourage you to avoid dismissive or vague language and give her the reverence she deserves.

Man, woman, masculine, feminine: I have done my best to acknowledge that sex, gender, love, relationships, and what are traditionally called masculine and feminine traits exist on a vast, ever-changing spectrum.

Although I believe that words matter, in the end, your understanding is not about the word. It is about your unique identity, what each word represents to you and the meaning you assign to it. I am a white, cisgender, heterosexual woman, and my personal stories are written from that perspective; please know, as you read this book, that I chose words with care, with the intention of being as inclusive and loving as I know how to be in this moment.

CHAPTER 1

WOMAN IN TOTAL CONSCIOUS HEALING

I am a *W.I.T.C.H.*

You, dear reader, are probably not all that fazed by the word *witch*. If you were, you wouldn't be reading this book. Most people, however, can't help but laugh nervously or tense up or flinch. Some make lame jokes—"So you, like, ride a broomstick and cast evil spells on the weekends and stuff?"—or change the subject.

Over the years, I've become acutely aware of the discomfort this word causes. In fact, the word used to make me uncomfortable. I, too, associated it with dancing naked in the moonlight and cackling over cauldrons and wearing black robes and generally being weird. Then I started to question that judgment. What's wrong with dancing naked, cackling, being weird? Who gets to say what the word *witch* even means? As I embarked on my healing journey, I became more aware of my psychic gifts and true nature, and I began to study other definitions of this word and why it's been used against women—especially women who don't like to follow rules that subjugate them—for centuries.

A few years ago, a male friend asked me why I have a certain painting prominently displayed above my desk. It's my favorite piece of art, a beautiful blush watercolor painting of a naked woman with long flowing hair flying on a broomstick, cheekily titled *BYE!*

I explained that I love it not only for its aesthetic appeal but also because I identify with what it represents—being a W.I.T.C.H., a woman who embraces her witchy powers and who has the courage to embody and be seen in all of it.

What I didn't add is that, for me, being a W.I.T.C.H. means being in touch with my psychic and energetic powers. I didn't feel the need to mention that I am a healer and a wise woman, a woman who is sensual and sexual and in sync with the phases of the moon and nature's continuous cycles of birth, life, death, and rebirth. That I get to choose how to show up in this world as a Woman in Total Conscious Healing for myself and for all the women who have come before me and for those who will follow. That would have probably been TMI.

"But why do you have to choose to call yourself a witch?" he asked. "Can't you choose something more palatable?"

And there it was, the patriarchy in one sentence. This term, with all its connotations, was too much, too weird, and too threatening. But I don't call myself a W.I.T.C.H. to be palatable—I call myself a W.I.T.C.H. because it's true.

Long before I dared to call myself a W.I.T.C.H., my parents immigrated to Germany, from Ireland and Scotland, in 1978. My family then moved from where I was born, in Aichwald, to a small town about thirty minutes farther south called Eislingen, nestled in a valley under the so-called three Kaiser mountains in the German region of Swabia. Originating with a small Roman castle in 125 BCE, Eislingen is now a rural suburb of twenty-two thousand souls that is divided into the predominantly Catholic north and Protestant south. Your religious affiliation determines a number of things, including which kindergarten you attend.

It was 1991. We'd moved there to have more space before my sister's entrance into this world; we were about to be a family of five. I officially became the middle child, between her and my older brother. My father built and ran his own plastering business, and my mother, after being a stay-at-home mom for a while, ran her own English tutoring school in town.

I was seven years old and had just started *Grundschule*, or primary school. I was the cerebral type, an observer who stood back and analyzed everything around me, trying to make sense of it and sometimes getting lost in a daydream. I tried everything from ballet to soccer, jazz dance to track and field, and I could never figure out why I ought to point my toes or run in circles. When reflecting on this time, my mother often says, "If I'd had to guess which of my children would be an Olympian, it certainly would not have been Siobhan."

As luck (or Divine intervention) would have it, a friend invited me to her fencing practice one day, and I instantly fell in love with the sport. Fencing requires attention to detail, patience, dedication, discipline, and self-control. Most importantly, it requires the ability to strategize, to be a step ahead of your opponent. This was my comfort zone, a place in which I could observe and analyze. Over time, with age and lots of practice, I grew to love the physicality of it as well. Little did I know that fencing would bring about many amazing experiences and also lead me down a path of heartache, uncertainty, opportunity, and lots of growth.

Soon I was training every night of the week and, when I could, during my lunch hour. My days looked something like this:

- 6:00 a.m.: Wake up, get showered and dressed, eat breakfast
- 6:45 a.m.: Catch the bus for a thirty-minute ride into the next town for school
- 7:30 a.m.: Attend school
- 12:30 p.m. to 2:00 p.m.: Take lunch break, during which I usually squeezed in a fencing lesson or homework
- 2:00 to 4:00 p.m.: Attend more school
- 4:00 to 5:30 p.m.: Catch the bus back home to change, grab a snack, and head to practice
- 6:30 to 9:00 p.m.: Attend fencing practice
- 9:00 to 11:00 p.m.: Shower, eat, study, and pass out
- Rinse and repeat

At first a hobby, fencing became an athletic career when I started competing internationally at the age of fourteen. In typical overachiever fashion, I competed not only in my own age group, which was Cadet (under sixteen), but also in two age classes above mine, including Junior (under nineteen) and Senior (nineteen and above). I loved being good at something and being recognized for it by my coaches, in our town, and by my family—especially my father.

My father was a big supporter of my fencing. Sports was one of the main ways he could relate to me and my siblings. I remember him taking me to a nearby fencing World Cup competition when I was about nine years old. I watched the competitors with complete awe; they were so elegant and powerful, masters of a craft I had just started to learn and love. I especially remember the sounds of maraging steel blades clinking, scoreboards beeping, and fencers screaming to underscore their touches. Passion, confidence, strength, competition, and tension filled the fencing hall. Afterward, I met and got an autograph from Anja Fichtel, who had won the gold at the 1988 Olympics in Seoul. I knew she was famous, but I didn't quite understand the Olympics yet. "I just started fencing," I told her.

"Keep practicing," she said. And so I did.

Children are like sponges, absorbing the ways in which our parents and other prominent adult figures in our lives respond to us. We adapt and learn how to regulate ourselves to behave and perform in order to elicit the love and approval we crave and actually need in the most basic sense. In my case, I learned early on that if I just kept to myself as much as possible, didn't rock the boat, and performed well at school and fencing, I would get that essential praise and attention. Although that approach worked for the most part, I didn't realize that when we regulate our own behaviors and emotions in an attempt to manage a caregiver's response, like vying for recognition or avoiding being yelled at, we neglect our own sense of self. We neglect getting to know our own emotions and needs and how to use our voice. If we don't know our own needs, we can't express them and therefore don't believe that they actually will be met. We learn to swallow our emotions and silence our voices.

My life revolved around school and fencing. It wasn't easy, and I had to sacrifice a lot, but I got to travel all over the world to compete in a sport I loved. Although much of my drive was born out of that love, it went much deeper than that. Anyone who was raised by immigrant parents will be able to relate. Hard work is your currency and therefore your means of survival. My parents made sure to instill that in us.

I am immensely grateful for my work ethic and for everything my parents did to help my brother, my sister, and me achieve our goals, but I do wish that I had also learned the importance of rest. Since my parents hardly had any time to themselves or to rest, we didn't get to have much idle time either—at least not without being made to feel guilty about it. And I, as the people pleaser, fully adopted being busy all the time in an effort to please. To this day, I feel guilty when I rest or enjoy too much idle time.

The desire to please, to strive to win love, and to ignore the body and its needs are part of my core wound, or *witch wound*, which manifests in subtle and not-so-subtle ways. Whenever I get sick, I end up with a sore throat or bronchitis. In the Western interpretation of the yogic chakra system as we know it today, there are seven energy centers along the spine from the pelvic floor to the crown of the head. Each represents a physical, energetic, and metaphorical/spiritual/psychological locus. The throat chakra, or energy center, is connected to authentic expression, and my propensity for experiencing "dis-ease" in this area, I believe, is an energetic and physical manifestation of stored memories and trauma, of a pattern of not speaking and living my truth. In moments of vulnerability or fear, I feel restriction in my throat, as if words won't form to leave my mouth, like I am being strangled or suffocated. I still carry a fear of rocking the boat and, as a recovering people pleaser, a tendency to fawn that I have to keep in check. It still doesn't feel natural for me to rest when I need it. I'm still reluctant to offer a differing opinion, and I'm hyperaware of the possibility of being called out as a fraud or impostor or loudmouth. I'm afraid that if I speak my truth, I'll lose everything. That I won't be safe.

THE WITCH WOUND

The way my witch wound expresses itself is common. Though your upbringing and early experiences might be drastically different from mine, you likely recognize some of those adaptive behaviors and fears. This is something many women share, and for good reason. For millennia, we've had to stay under the radar in order to survive.

The witch trials, both the three-hundred-year period of religious-based persecution in Europe and Colonial America and the short, violent stint in 1692–93 in Salem, were, at their core, a centuries-long effort to suppress any sort of threat to the church and to those who benefited from its ideology. Women, as well as some men, who dared to speak freely or express disagreement with the men in charge, who owned property, who were deemed too sexual by Puritan standards, whose hair was too red, who were in tune with nature and the moon, who refused to be cowed in one form or another, or who were simply in the wrong place at the wrong time—these people were called witches and jailed and starved and hanged and drowned and burned.

That was the most extreme version of witch persecution. More often, women who are of service to other women or to a feminist agenda—which is, simply put, working toward equality—or who have some kind of economic or social power are targeted in insidious but less violent ways. These women include herbalists, midwives, wisewomen, and healers, as well as activists, politicians, teachers, artists, and executives—those who authentically express their truth and rail against the status quo, or who have enough money and status to flout the rules.

And so we are all living with the witch wound. Also known as the persecution wound, it is our collective spiritual trauma, carried forward through generations by our ancestors, from our own past lives in which we were persecuted, or in our daily brushes with ongoing social and systemic oppression. No matter where or whom we come from, there's a good chance that the effects of thousands of years of misogyny live on in us, in our very DNA. The legitimate fear of punishment and violence carries on in the form of the witch wound. It is a wound that stems from the invalidation and suppression of our innate feminine gifts—our intuition, our sensuality, our embodiment, our psychic powers—as well as the danger in our daily lives as women.

The witch wound manifests in many different ways and often subconsciously. Many of us are afraid to speak up, to share ourselves openly and freely, to try something new and risk making a mistake, or to draw attention to ourselves. Our nervous systems are turned up to eleven. Many of us will do just about anything to gain approval, even if it means working from before dawn to way past dusk and hiding behind a socially acceptable front, completely detached from our true self, our true thoughts and needs and desires. We play small, don't take up too much space, are quiet, likable, and palatable. To avoid being killed, abused, or silenced, we disavow the Divine feminine.

TOXIC FEMININITY AND MASCULINITY

The yoga of spiritual intimacy celebrates the polarity principles of masculine/feminine, light/dark, emptiness/fullness, and structure/ flow that guide the cosmos as pathways to passion, play, and divine union.

—John Wineland

Together, we can shed light on how the values of patriarchal systems became so ingrained in society, as well as on how we protect the witch wound with shiny armor, a false self that we believe will keep us safe. But this armor actually traps us inside a world of fear and the internalized voice of disapproval. Our minds create even more fearful stories to validate these false beliefs, and continue to feed the fear until we turn against ourselves. This armor often takes the form of toxic femininity and masculinity.

The only way to change our way of being and the toxic ways of relating to one another is to address this wound with compassion and humility. It is the mission of the modern-day W.I.T.C.H. to bring the nearly forgotten energy of the Divine feminine to the world in an effort to restore balance for all beings.

Please note that by "feminine" and "masculine," I am not referring to sex or gender, men or women, but rather polarizing energies that exist in each of us. It's a spectrum, or a circle, without hierarchy. Feminine energy is yin, Shakti, internally focused, creative, related to the right brain, and associated with the moon. Masculine energy is yang, Shiva, externally focused, structured, related to the left brain, and associated with the sun.

In a patriarchy, which is all about binaries and hierarchies, masculinity is valued over femininity. Action is valued over contemplation, strength over softness, logic over intuition, work over rest. Our reward systems reflect as much, but in an inconsistent and confusing way. Many women are rewarded for masculine energy in the professional or athletic realm, for hard work and discipline, as long as it's presented in a nice, tidy, feminine package. As long as women burn the candle at both ends with a pleasant lipsticked smile on our faces, we're acceptable. Our male colleagues, meanwhile, are rewarded as long as they work hard, keep their hair short and their ties straight, and limit their feminine traits to displays of corporate-mandated workplace sensitivity. Sometimes they are paid more for doing the same job. Of course, everyone suffers under this conditioning.

Women and men as well as nonbinary and queer folx must navigate the nebulous line between genders and the performative traits associated with them. Strong versus soft. Quiet versus assertive. Focused versus open. Certain versus curious. Decisive versus flexible. Calculating versus creative. Stoic versus emotional. And so on ad infinitum.

Taken to an extreme, when someone leans too far in one direction—as we are all trained to do—these traits can turn toxic. Rest becomes depression. Assertiveness becomes mansplaining. Flexibility lies down and takes the form of a doormat. Stoicism transforms into neurotic repression, numbness, even antipathy or sociopathy. Quiet becomes silenced. Strength mutates into aggression, coercion, or violence. Intuitiveness becomes untethered, self-centered, even solipsistic.

We see these expressions in subtle and not-so-subtle ways all the time. My grandmother used to say, "Keep your airs and graces about you." You might have been told to "act like a lady." Such statements perpetuate toxic femininity by reducing our expression to socially acceptable behaviors like not being overly assertive or emotional. I was also once told, "You can be successful, but you will be lonely. You can't have both." This implied that being independent and successful would make me undesirable for a "real man," who expects a woman to be subservient. This is an example of both toxic masculinity and toxic femininity.

As a society, we have toxic systemic imbalances to fix. Calling out structures and behaviors that are abusive or discriminatory serves all of us, though some people who benefit from their perceived superior position, from their ability to successfully perform perceived superior traits, or from their connection to privilege will undoubtedly feel threatened. And being the one to do the calling out is undoubtedly dangerous. Would you personally give up $30,000 for income equity? Would you risk losing a promotion in order to expose sexual harassment in your office?

Raising awareness about structures that have existed for

eons and have empowered men to possess physical and social advantages isn't an easy feat. Simply taking up more space, speaking our truth, or sharing personal experiences of bias, injustice, abuse, or discrimination can elicit backlash. We might decide to push back against the status quo out in the world, or we might not. Each of us has to make that choice for ourselves. Either way, every one of us can notice our own toxic traits, ask how we are contributing to the cycle of toxic relating, and do the deeper work to change our patterns. We have to notice how these traits express themselves in our lives instead of simply reacting from our reptilian brain in fight-or-flight mode. Because we live in an inherently unequal society, in which the Divine feminine feels like a threat to the patriarchy and the disembodied masculine world, we have to weigh the pros and cons of action, personal change, and personal risk.

What if we were allowed to cultivate and express feminine and masculine traits, to find our personal and unique balance? What if we dismantled the value system, if we stopped designating certain traits as good or bad? How do we, as Women in Total Conscious Healing, get to a place where we realize our own true power and claim our freedom of self-expression?

TRY THIS: UNCOVERING YOUR TOXIC TRAITS

STEP 1:

Do some research on toxic masculinity and femininity. Identify where these traits show up in your life and where you have subscribed to these beliefs and behaviors, as shown in the example below. As always, awareness is the first step.

My worth is my productivity.

STEP 2:

Ask yourself where these beliefs originated—from family, friends, media, work, et cetera.

> *I absorbed toxic productivity from my family, because . . . but also from our capitalistic society.*

STEP 3:

Get curious about your beliefs and your behaviors. Ask yourself:

- Which of these beliefs belong to me? Which beliefs did I absorb from others around me?
- Are my behaviors and actions truly what are best for me? Am I acting a certain way because I am expected to?

STEP 4:

Validate your feelings and your experiences. As a collective, men and women are asked to invalidate or minimize experiences and feelings. Make it a point to take the time to be with your feelings and validate them. Tell yourself: "My feelings matter" or "It is normal to feel this way and to want to cry."

> *It is OK to rest and to not feel guilty about it.*

> *I am enough simply for existing and being me.*
> *I don't have to do or produce to deserve love.*

STEP 5:

Practice responding in ways that feel authentic to you and make space to explore new perspectives, beliefs, and behaviors.

- Schedule breaks in your day to take a walk or meditate.
- Leave your weekend without plans and allow room for flow and creativity to emerge.
- Say no to obligations or projects that aren't actually what you want to be doing.

HEALING THE WITCH WOUND

There came a point in my life, right around my Saturn return, when I was extremely successful on paper, but I was feeling depressed, isolated, and lost. This is a classic Saturn return, which happens approximately every twenty-eight to thirty years, the time it takes for Saturn to return to the exact zodiac sign and degree it was in when a person was born. It's a potent astrological transit, a wake-up call, a summons to slow down and go inward, to reflect on your life choices and your soul's purpose. The big stuff. This is why Saturn is also referred to as the teacher of the zodiac.

Before my Saturn return, I don't think that I had ever really asked myself who I was or what I wanted from life. I'd avoided those hard questions by drowning myself in work and achievement. But now, building my own life in NYC, making my own money, and no longer needing to answer to my parents or my coaches, I was ready. I was twenty-nine and right on time.

Since then, over the last decade, I have been guided to awaken, to take an honest look at my reality, and to redefine what it means to be a woman and to be successful. I am trying to figure out what I want from this lifetime and what I want to pass on to the next generation. I am trying to heal my witch wound.

And so I set out on a journey to explore what lived underneath the armor that I had built to keep me safe and successful by patriarchal societal standards. Chasing achievements and trying to perfectly live up to the expectations of others, as well as my own, was plain exhausting.

I knew there had to be a greater purpose than the one I was living.

In the mid-twentieth century, American psychologist Abraham Maslow theorized about the motivation to find purpose and the process of self-improvement once your most basic needs are met, which came to be known as Maslow's hierarchy of needs. The first order of business are the physiological needs of food, water, and generally healthy bodily function, followed by basic safety and security, love and belonging within social or family structures, the esteem of peers and the confidence to pursue goals, and, last, self-actualization. I had climbed the bottom two steps of the pyramid by having access to nourishing food, clean water, and stable housing; by taking care of my body and health; by establishing myself in my career; and by saving enough money for an emergency fund. I had also accumulated more achievements than I could ever fit on my résumé. At the end of the day, however, I didn't fully feel like I belonged, or that my achievements could be translated to a more actualized sense of self. Our deepest desire, I realized, is to be loved.

We are born open, completely receptive, a manifestation of pure love. Over time we get hurt, become confused, face karmic life lessons, and build thick and high walls to hide behind. We get stuck in our minds and identify with our fear-based ego self. We resist the love that is available to us always and without conditions out of fear of being hurt.

Eventually, we arrive at a place where we realize that the love we so deeply crave comes from within, that we have become disconnected from our true nature but long to be at home in our bodies. Yet this knowledge is only one step toward loving ourselves, after a lifetime of listening to the internalized voice of disapproval. The habits of belittling ourselves with constant negative self-talk, holding ourselves to unrealistic perfectionist standards, pushing ourselves to achieve "success," and resisting receiving what we actually want and desire can be hard to break, especially if we don't believe that we deserve to break them. If we don't believe that we truly deserve love.

Oh, how I have fallen into this trap. I constantly push myself, wanting to do everything on my own and accepting nothing less than the best results. My inner critic has been a close companion for as long as I can remember. A part of me recognizes her role in my accomplishments and successes—and I thank her for keeping me motivated when I was ready to give up and when things got hard. But the wiser and softer part of me realizes how damaging that inner voice has been and that I let her run too much of my life for too long, that her motivation came from a place of lack and avoidance, a fear of failure and abandonment.

Where along the way did we forget our true nature? How and when did it start to feel unsafe to be soft, gentle, in flow with the cyclical rhythm of creation and life itself? At what point did we decide to criticize and push ourselves, to harden our soft hearts? When did we start to believe that controlling our circumstances would keep us safe and comfortable?

The fact is that pain and discomfort are unavoidable and essential parts of our spiritual journey. Change is simply part of that journey; there is so much in life and the Universe that we are not in control of—actually, most of it. Yet we spend our lives worrying, hiding, and trying to control, and all we end up doing is restricting the flow of life. We cut off the life-force energy that wants to move through us.

What we try to avoid at all costs is what can actually bring us closer to ourselves. A painful experience, something that gets at our core wounds, is what will eventually crack those thick walls. Going through a bad breakup, losing a loved one, getting fired, being rejected, losing a home and sense of security, receiving a tough diagnosis, being defeated at the Olympics. The key is to get to a point in our spiritual journey where we no longer try to build a thicker, sturdier wall in reaction to loss or hurt but instead have the courage to let the light shine through the cracks that pain brings to illuminate that which wants to be set free.

As I was turning my attention inward and learning to love and accept myself more, I began craving that deep, scary, almost painful connection that I know is possible—with a partner but also, most importantly, with myself. I knew that I could no longer avoid uncomfortable feelings and shunned parts of myself, that I had to discover my edges and push past them.

As this process unfurled, I found a new edge: coming out of the spiritual closet, particularly in the realm of dating. Showing up as the woman I was becoming as a result of my conscious work and healing required me to push past my core rejection and abandonment wounds and to move beyond the more palatable roles of corporate executive and Olympic athlete to expose the witchy, dark-feminine, and sexual parts of myself.

At first, I would play a role until I could get an idea of how open-minded my date was, until I thought it was safe to share more about myself. Later, I swung the pendulum far to the other side, boldly announcing "I am a psychic" on my dating profile, hoping to weed out anyone threatened by that. This did not work.

Instead, people reacted rather than engaged. They didn't

seem to be all that curious about what being psychic or spiritual meant, or what it meant to me, instead asking hokey questions like "What am I thinking right now?" or simply dismissing or belittling me with statements like "That's not real" or "I don't believe you can talk to someone's grandma." To my dismay, announcing myself as a psychic did not prevent rejection.

I believe that I have lived many previous lives as women who had no choice but to hide their gifts and be palatable or risk being killed or ostracized. But this life is different. I know that this time around, I am here to live out my truth, my authentic self, no matter how scary or uncomfortable it may be at times. I am healing my wound of being "too much" or "not lovable" or "weird," and no matter how painful some of my lessons may be, they are just what I need to push past my edges, to go to new depths within, and to love, nurture, accept, and express myself.

Your karmic lessons can soften and empower you at the same time. All it takes is the courage to sit with the pain and the grief and to allow them to crack your heart open without erecting another wall. Then you will do it all again. You will crave an even deeper connection, go to even scarier depths, and become even more powerfully aligned.

In my opinion, in order to heal our witch wounds, we need to make a concerted effort to connect with the Divine feminine to create a more balanced way of relating to ourselves and others. I believe that true magic happens when we balance the masculine and feminine aspects of ourselves. Most of us have gone so far "yang" that we need a hefty dose of "yin" to counter it. Finding your unique center might take some trial and error.

For me, it wasn't until I was able to slowly relinquish some of my armor, my overly masculine style of work—toxic productivity—and my stoic ways of relating that I started to feel more empowered from the inside out. I now actively practice not always pushing myself to do more or fill up every single slot on my schedule: to not work out every single day, to not overly control my food intake or monitor my weight and appearance, to not master my to-do list, to not numb out all my feelings, and to not live up to everyone's expectations. Softening and surrendering, however, come with their own challenges. Leaning too far into my feminine can have a negative impact on my physical and mental health. Feeling, desiring, and dreaming need to be backed up with aligned action. Resting too much and for too long can turn into inertia. The key is to know when to ramp up the masculine, when to soften into the feminine, and to accept all traits as good and equal in moderation.

True freedom is choosing to embody both the masculine and the feminine, to be honest with ourselves about our heart's true desires, and to freely express our inner truths on behalf of not only our own transformation but the transformation of the collective.

Will this be easy? Certainly not. Choosing to heed the call and go down a path of spiritual awakening is not for the faint of heart. Choosing to forge your own path, the path of a Woman in Total Conscious Healing, is even harder. Can we find the courage to allow the flow of divinity? Can we share our voices and our beliefs in ways that allow the voices and beliefs of others to exist? Can we express our own unique gifts for the good of all?

Doing so requires us to face what we keep hidden and to become very uncomfortable and vulnerable. It requires confronting our inner demons, the pain we tuck away in order to avoid it. Not feeling will not keep us safe, however, and contorting our identities, behaviors, and our environment will only keep us disconnected from our true selves and from living a desire-led life.

Life is to be lived and experienced. Love is accessible

always, because at our core we are love. It is our job to become aware and to remember. This is the practice and the healing journey . . . to peel back the layers and allow the energy to flow, no matter how uncomfortable it may be at times. This is self-love, and this is true freedom.

CLAIMING W.I.T.C.H.

The world continues to be dangerous for women in so many ways, but we have more power and resources at our fingertips than ever before, at least in this Western and capitalistic part of the world and in this precious moment. Still, why would we choose to call ourselves W.I.T.C.H., or witches, when the word is so scary to so many people? Of course, we can't take for granted that we are privileged today in that we can not only call ourselves witches but also embody our true nature and share our gifts with the world. Even so, some—many—still do feel threatened by it, still judge and criticize us, still work strenuously to limit our rights and personal autonomy, still tell us to shut up and get back in the kitchen where we belong. Some perpetrate violence against us, not necessarily because of a label but because of basic misogyny, of simple hatred (fear) of women.

That is why it is up to those of us who can claim our power with little fear of actual violence or loss of basic security to do so, to claim W.I.T.C.H.

In the *Oxford Dictionary of Phrase and Fable*, a witch is defined as "a person, typically a woman, who practises magic or sorcery and was traditionally thought to have evil magic powers; such witches are popularly depicted as wearing a black cloak and pointed hat, and flying on a broomstick . . ."

Modern witches do indeed have magical powers, but we don't usually wear pointed hats and black cloaks, except on Halloween. We look like, and are, anyone: corporate consultants in suits, Pilates teachers in athleisure gear, middle-school principals in friendly sweaters, lawyers, artists, carpenters, business owners, doctors, mail carriers, parents, the barista who just handed you that scrumptious caramel latte. Some use the word *witch* to describe themselves; some don't. Ultimately, it isn't about the word we use, but what it represents and what we are taking back.

As written in *Witchcraft: The Library of Esoterica*, the witch archetype is only one embodied representation of the Divine feminine among many other archetypes. These archetypes are in constant evolution as we evolve as women and as a collective, as we reclaim the ancient practices of matriarchal worship and goddess cultures. We can all be witches by seeking self-realization, connection with our community, and creative expression—our craft. Simply put, the witch archetype today embodies the rise against centuries of oppression.

The first time I publicly called myself a W.I.T.C.H. was in February 2020. I had signed up to take a five-day intensive workshop with Fearless Communicators, a public speaking–coaching business committed to elevating women's voices and amplifying the reach and impact of their messages. It was during this process, while creating my keynote speech, that I got the clear download of the acronym *W.I.T.C.H.*, for Women in Total Conscious Healing, which became the title of my keynote and the concept for this book. During my final presentation, to an invited audience of close to seventy-five people, I asked everyone to stand up and say after me: *"I am a W.I.T.C.H.!"* It was powerful and freeing. After the presentation, my dear friend Renee came up to me and said, "You provided a lot of healing to people tonight by sharing your story and calling yourself a witch in public. You healed a part of me."

Let's use and elevate the word *W.I.T.C.H.*, to reclaim it as an act of healing the generational trauma of the women and men before us who were persecuted for living out their innate powers and being their true selves.

As Women in Total Conscious Healing, it is part of our curriculum to uncover why we fear what we fear, to ask why something feels unsafe, not just logically but in our bodies and our psyches, and to listen to what it is that we need to feel safe. Coming out of the spiritual closet, living authentically, and becoming fully embodied will certainly take you to your edge over and over again. It will fire up your nervous system and at times make you want to crawl out of your skin, but it is the only way to really step into your true self and your true power. We are magical, powerful, emotional, and intuitive creatrices, and it is our time to walk this earth as who we were born to be. Women in Total Conscious Healing—when *you* rise, we *all* rise.

REFLECTION

- What is your relationship to the word *witch*? What were you taught about witches?
- Can you identify your witch wound (or wounds)? In what ways does it manifest in your life?
- What were you taught about being a woman (by society, religion, family)? How does it feel to be a woman?
- What does masculinity and femininity mean to you? Do you currently exhibit the toxic version of any of their traits?
- What are some of the beliefs you hold on to from your upbringing? Which of these are no longer valid or don't ring true for you? Is there a reason you are still holding on to them?

- Are your life choices dictated by fear? Does fear control your outlook on life and your attitude? Are these fears valid? If not, what can you do to overcome these fears?
- What are you most passionate about? Are you taking steps toward following your passion? If not, what is preventing you from exploring your passion?
- Do you like yourself and the life you are living? If not, what don't you like and why? What steps are you taking toward changing your situation?
- What does conscious healing mean to you?

Go check out my speech "Elixir for Becoming a Woman in Total Conscious Healing" at www.siobhanclaire.com/speaking -engagements.

CHAPTER 2

CHANGE IS PART OF YOUR STORY

Make friends with change.

—*Ram Dass*

All my hard work and hours upon hours spent training at the fencing club paid off, and by the time I turned seventeen, I was ranked fourth in the world for Juniors. It was 2001. Just as I had clawed my way to the top, however, I would experience one of the first tipping points that would completely change the trajectory of my life.

I was born and raised in Germany, as I mentioned, but I am an Irish citizen and an Irish passport holder. I do not hold dual citizenship because I was born before the year 2000, at which point Germany started to grant citizenship to children born in Germany even if their parents weren't German passport holders. That meant that once I was ready to compete internationally, I had to represent Ireland instead of Germany. I had never even thought about my nationality as more than a passport I needed to travel, but once I became more success-ful, people started paying attention to this designation.

My club coach was promoted to be the German national coach for my discipline of women's saber, and all of a sudden we had a conflict of interest on our hands. Having a highly ranked student was part of the equation for keeping his title and remaining the German national coach for seasons to come, but the fact that I wasn't representing Germany on the international circuit did not help his case. In an attempt to re-solve the situation, he and the German Fencing Federation ap-proached me and asked me to change my nationality so I could officially compete for Germany. My family and I seriously con-sidered all options, but I was not allowed to renounce my Irish citizenship until the age of eighteen. Further complicating the situation was the fact that I would have faced a temporary ban from competing by choosing to switch countries, right before the qualifying period for the 2004 Olympics, in Athens. My hands were tied.

Once I turned eighteen, the pressure to change my nation-ality started bordering on harassment. I had a physical reac-tion to this, but I didn't know how to listen to my body in the way I know now. I felt sick to my stomach, anxious, and con-fused. I spent most of the time in a daze, trying to cope with the emotional torment while facing a very tough decision. I became fixated on trying to control the outcome, minimizing conflict, and pleasing all parties involved. I was tortured by questions. *What should I do? Whom do I disappoint? Whom do I owe my loyalty to? What is the best decision for the long term? How could my success suddenly turn against me?*

Even though my body, with its emotional intelligence, was firing on all cylinders as it tried to guide me, I wasn't able to recognize or trust my own truth because I spent much of my life relying on the opinions and reactions of others to dictate my reality. I wavered in a state of indecisiveness for way too long, causing myself unnecessary torment.

Of course, there came a point when I was forced to make a decision. The obvious self-serving actions of the German Fencing Federation and my club coach pushed me away from aligning my interests with theirs, and so I took a leap of faith and decided to continue to represent Ireland. I knew that making this decision would disappoint certain people, but I couldn't have imagined the extent of the resulting ostracism, further confirming my belief that people wouldn't respect, support, or meet my needs.

My club coach stopped working with me, and my club didn't provide alternative solutions, like letting me train with another coach. Many of my club mates and friends jumped on the bandwagon. Some stopped talking to me completely, and some even made comments such as "Why don't you go back to where you came from?" News flash: I came from the same small town they did.

This was devastating, especially as I was about to enter the 2004 Olympic qualifying season. Anyone who has been an athlete understands the importance of the coaching relationship and the level of trust that is necessary to be successful as a team. For most young adults, first heartbreak comes from dating, but for me it came when I got dumped by my coach.

Before this, I'd never considered myself "other." I was born and raised in Germany, fully assimilated in every aspect of my life. True, I had an Irish name, and my mother had an accent, but so what?

Now, all perceived differences had been made clear to me. I took it very personally. I didn't understand why my club mates thought my decision was selfish or disloyal. I didn't understand or wasn't able to accept that my coach was reacting out of fear of losing his job. Just as it wasn't my responsibility to be a pawn in his career trajectory, it wasn't his responsibility to put my plans before his. Both sides had untenable expectations of the student-coach relationship and our roles in it, all while losing sight of who we were and the bigger picture of the path we were on.

If I could learn to welcome change as part of my story, then I could gain perspective, let go of what "should be," and allow myself to be guided toward something better. And so I was about to start my final year in gymnasium (German high school) and facing the 2004 Olympic qualifying year without a coach and within a toxic training environment. I had two options: give up and walk away or dig deep. I decided to dig deep, and I mean really deep. Looking back at this time of my life now, I am amazed at how tough I was and how much perseverance was already within me. I didn't know it at the time, but I was being prepared to learn about my own strengths as well as my limitations.

I was determined to not let anyone nullify my years of hard work and take away my opportunity to qualify for the Olympics. The trials were set for April 2004, right before my final exams. In preparation, I trained with a personal trainer, took fencing lessons from a club in the next town over, and— believe it or not—still showed up to practice at my original club despite the bullying just so I could have sparring time. I no longer traveled to competitions with my club and the German team; I was now traveling to international competitions by myself. All while studying for my exams.

The stress was intense, but I had tunnel vision. I had no clue what would happen after April. *Would I qualify for the Olympics? Would I keep fencing? Where would I go to college? When would I even find the time to apply?* Little did I know that I would get my answers much sooner than I thought—or, better, right on time.

The year before, at the Senior World Fencing Championships in Havana, Cuba, two unexpected opportunities had presented themselves to me. In the very small world of elite fencing, word about my circumstances had made its way around the circuit. Much to my surprise, the French national coach offered for me to come study in Paris and train with the French national team after graduation. The second offer came from the man whom I now call my coach, Vladimir Nazlymov, one of the greatest saber fencers in his own time. His reputation preceded him, and I had known about him way before he sat down next to me in the stands. Right then and there, he recruited me to be part of the fencing team at the Ohio State University. Knowing that I wasn't always going to be alone and that there were options for me to continue fencing after I graduated from high school had given me some momentum to keep pushing toward my goal of qualifying for the Olympics.

Now, six months later, I was on the train to Belgium to compete at the Athens Olympic qualifiers. My entire being was filled with determination. I was also worried. Everything was different from what I had imagined. *Had I done enough to prepare? Was I ready? What if I didn't prove those who'd abandoned me wrong? What if I failed?*

The next day, I fought my way to the semifinals but lost my bout and the chance to compete for gold. However, since the top three fencers would qualify for the Olympics, I still had one last chance by fighting for bronze. After a very close match against my opponent from Ukraine, I ended up losing 15–13, narrowly missing qualification by two points. So close but oh so far . . . another four years to be exact. I was heartbroken and exhausted, physically and emotionally. I questioned whether everything I had put myself through had been worth it, whether I truly had another four years in me, knowing I would have to keep digging even deeper. I honestly didn't know if I could do it.

There went my plan.

I could have walked away from fencing at that moment, but I recognize now that I was presented with options for a reason. If that wasn't my path, then I would have been guided in a different direction, and I don't think it would have mattered if I had chosen Paris or Columbus; what mattered was that I took the leap into the unknown.

After the Olympic qualifiers, I took a break from fencing to focus on finishing high school. I spent the summer a complete nervous wreck, trying to cope with all the emotions swirling through my being. I was still dealing with the heartbreak of a broken dream and the exhaustion from the last two years, while trying to prepare myself for the impending departure from life as I knew it. I remember the week leading up to my move to the US. Saying my goodbyes to friends, then my boyfriend of two years, and finally my family. That was by far one of the hardest times for me, because I knew that my life would never be the same and I was starting a new chapter—alone, and far, far away.

And I did it. I left my family and friends. I traveled across the world to start school in a foreign city where I knew no one. I moved to the US without any guarantee of the outcome.

I spent the next four years studying, training three to five hours a day, and traveling to competitions in the US as well as internationally. I didn't exactly have a "normal" college experience, and despite enduring another toxic coaching relationship, my fencing team became my family. Somehow I managed to be a straight A student and a four-time all-American—hello, overachiever—and to prepare for the Olympics.

WELCOMING CHANGE

Inner peace is:
feeling and being with your emotions without
reacting to them; it is the calmness that emerges
when you embrace change.

—*Yung Pueblo*

As we set out on our life's journey, we are often tricked by what we think life *should* look like. We attach expectations to ourselves, to others, and to situations based on our perception and conditioning. We have this illusion that *when* we achieve or obtain something—usually something that's based on some external rubric—*then* we will be happy, loved, or deserving. And when life doesn't pan out the way we planned or imagined, then we doubt ourselves and see it as a failure. That's only natural. I wanted, more than just about anything, for my coach to support me, for my teammates to like and respect me, and to qualify for the Olympics. And when I didn't, my entire vision of my life fell away, and I was left heart-hurt and floundering.

This bend in the road wasn't only about getting me to the Olympics; it was a stepping-stone for growth, for moving out of the fishbowl of Eislingen and toward spiritual awakening. Perhaps I always knew deep down that I was a true cosmopolitan and would have to eventually break out of the confines of a small town and a small-town mentality to live a more global and expansive existence. Perhaps I didn't. Either way, what happened happened, and so I did the only thing I could do: I leaped into the unknown.

I often ask myself how I took a path so different from that of most people I know. How did I set out toward this Olympic feat?

I remember watching the opening ceremonies of the 2000 Olympics in Sydney. At this point, I had already been competing on the international circuit for two years, so I actually knew a few of the fencers who were competing. This was the first time I had a personal connection to this event, and it no longer seemed so unattainable. I remember thinking to myself, *If they can do it, then why can't I?* This was when a fantasy became an actual goal.

I had released an intention into the Universe without really knowing what I was doing. I didn't know when, how, or if it would happen, and I certainly could have never foreseen the many obstacles and twists along the way. There were many times when I could have chosen to quit fencing or decided not to try out for the Olympics, but, for whatever reason, I just kept following the bread crumbs as they led me to new places, new people, and new situations. I simply continued to take action toward the goal, not realizing that each step was also guiding me to experiences that would show me where I needed to grow.

The leap into the unknown is essential for learning about the unknown parts of yourself, because it's so much more difficult to heal and awaken if we stay surrounded by the energies that caused us to need healing in the first place. Sometimes we might take the long way around, but regardless of the path we choose, we will get to where we need to be to learn the lessons we signed up for in this lifetime.

That leap is not always easy. We have to go through hardship to understand the depths of ourselves. We need to let our lives as we know them crumble in order to see what we are left with, what truly matters. Then we can start to rebuild ourselves to be Women in Total Conscious Healing.

There is power in welcoming change as part of our story. Embracing change guides us to the right path, to people and experiences that will help us on our soul's growth journey.

Change broadens our perspectives and deepens our empathy for ourselves and others. It helps each of us grow and evolve to realize that we are no longer the same person, and that going back to a place we have outgrown is actually worse than moving toward a place where we can continue to discover ourselves, even if such a move feels scary. Change invites us to reflect on our growth, and to integrate the lessons we have been given. The leap into the unknown allows us to redefine ourselves and to explore more than just *one* way of doing life.

Anyway, change is going to happen, despite your opinions on the matter. So why not welcome it instead of fighting it? Why not approach change with an open mind and heart, with curiosity about where this next unexpected twist will take you? If you don't, resistance will only drain your energy. If you do, you'll have so much to give.

TRY THIS: STOP "SHOULD"-ING ON YOURSELF

"Should"-ing on yourself adds an immense amount of pressure; it is the ego's way of keeping us feeling inadequate. Let's become aware of how we "should" on ourselves.

STEP 1:

Write down all the "shoulds" that come to mind (e.g., "I really should have bought a house by now!"). Put your pen to paper and write; don't overthink it. Stop when you've exhausted all the "shoulds" that come to mind.

STEP 2:

Look at each statement you wrote and honestly ask: "Why?" Write down your answers.

Why should I have bought a house by now?
Because I am in my late thirties, and I am
wasting all this money on rent. Most people
my age already have a house and a family.

STEP 3:

Change all statements to start with: "If I really wanted to, I could . . ." Then ask yourself: "Why haven't I?" Write down your honest answer.

If I really wanted to, I could buy a house. I
haven't bought a house yet because I'm not
ready to leave NYC, and I cannot afford to buy
an apartment in NYC, nor would I do that. I
would prefer to buy a house when I am ready
to settle down and grow a family. I don't even
know where I would want to buy, and it hasn't
been the right time.

STEP 4:

Change all "shoulds" to positive statements and affirmations.

I am excited to buy the house I am meant to
buy, in the location I am meant to be in, when
the time is right. I trust that I will know when
that is.

This exercise helps you to be honest with yourself and realize that (a) you don't actually want to do what it takes to get a certain result, (b) you don't actually need to be pressuring yourself, because you are already working toward something, and (c) the outcome isn't realistic, or it simply isn't the right time. By reframing your "shoulds," you can take some of the unnecessary pressure off and embrace change as part of your process.

BREAKING THROUGH TOXIC PRODUCTIVITY

For me, a planner and someone who was raised to be an achiever and a doer, I have found that I don't easily arrive at a state of openness, welcoming change. I'd much, much rather resist, filling my life with busyness, with action for the sake of action. I'm much more comfortable in that state of doing. And, for the most part, I've always been rewarded for it. All my life I got praise for being able to do so much, for being able to juggle and balance school and competition, for "having it all under control," and for "being mature and independent." I got confirmation and reaffirmation that performing, meeting the expectations of others, and keeping everything perfectly together was a formula for "success" and for "being" the Siobhan that everyone wanted me to be.

In a capitalistic society, we glorify hard work and vilify rest. We call ourselves lazy for wanting to take a break. We are called unsuccessful or not driven if we don't want to kill ourselves to "climb the ladder" or if we aren't always chasing the next best thing. In corporate culture, we somehow aren't committed if we aren't willing to go the extra mile(s)—cue the work martyr. It has become a badge of honor to not have time to eat lunch, to not have time to step outside for some fresh air, to work late hours and on weekends. People "brag" about this behavior to show their commitment, hoping to advance. In reality, they fear that they will somehow fall behind or lose their identity.

The pandemic has only exacerbated this problem. All of a sudden, many of us had an unprecedented amount of free time, but instead of using that time to rest, recharge, and take care of our health and our relationships, many of us ended up working more. This pressure and need to perform and constantly be "doing" is robbing us of the journey called life, and it is preventing us from connecting to our being and desires.

It would be years before I recognized that this behavior celebrated in our society is toxic. What exactly constitutes toxic productivity? It is an unhealthy desire to feel productive at all times and at all costs. I am not talking just about work but also in your home life and your downtime. You can easily recognize if you suffer from toxic productivity when the pressure or guilt you feel to perform doesn't leave you even once you have completed a task or a project. No accomplishment is ever enough to squelch that sense of guilt, and there is hardly ever a feeling of fulfillment. You never stop to celebrate the process or the milestones along the way, and even if you do, it doesn't feel like an accomplishment. You feel like a failure if you aren't constantly doing something, and your focus is singular—you can only focus on what you need to do or what hasn't been accomplished, constantly judging and criticizing yourself and others. You feel like a failure if you don't have a plan.

All of this is a distraction. Too often we come to a crossroads and choose to do what we think we *should* do to meet expectations of others without understanding what is true for us, what is important to us, and what actually matters. This is the real waste of time. Instead of fearing falling behind on some imaginary timeline, fear wasting your time on forcing action, living your life for others, and setting the wrong priorities. Stopping and asking yourself, "What am I choosing to do right now—and why?" takes awareness, which sometimes only arrives at a sticking point. For me, I'd remember to pause and reflect only during times of true existential "stuck-ness" and frustration, times when I had tried everything and banged my head against the wall for far too long. That was when I encountered the invitation to surrender. It is in situations when I intuitively know something different has to happen or change, but realize that I cannot do what I want to do or change what I hope to change, that I remember I need to give it over to the Universe, albeit reluctantly at times.

TRY THIS: EMBRACING REST

Many cultures around the world embrace rest and self-care. In Denmark it is called hygge; in the Netherlands it's *niksen*. Wherever you are, you can learn to rest and do nothing without shame or guilt.

STEP 1:

Start small by scheduling breaks of a few minutes throughout the day, and work yourself up to a few hours at a time.

STEP 2:

Be purposeful and use these scheduled breaks to take a few deep breaths, and just be with your breath, without needing to change anything or distract yourself. This might take some practice, and might feel uncomfortable at first, but stick with it and you will soon notice the positive effects on your nervous system and general stress level.

STEP 3:

Take this one step further: In precious moments of downtime, reframe your thoughts, and instead of asking yourself, "What should I be doing right now?" ask yourself, "What do I need right now?" or "What do I feel right now?" Then give yourself what you need without feeling guilty.

SPIRITUAL SURRENDER

"Surrender to the process" is something you hear a lot in the spiritual community. But what does it actually mean to surrender to the process, or to be in spiritual surrender? This is another concept that I couldn't understand until I had lived it. I am sure many of you struggle to embody this concept as well.

When we first start out on a spiritual path, the concept of surrender can seem very foreign, especially for those of us who like to be in control, to make plans, to call the shots. I for one love making plans, and don't get me wrong—I am not suggesting you should throw your planners out the window. What I am saying is that we end up getting in our own way when we fixate on plans and outcomes, when we try to control circumstances and resist the process, or the path. We hold on so tight because releasing the grip of our ego is scary, and we use plans to regulate our nervous systems and cope with existential fear. We want, more than anything, to manage the chaos.

Of course, we can't see the big picture, and the Universe laughs at the best-laid plans. Or, as Allen Saunders was famously quoted as saying in *Reader's Digest* in 1957, "Life is what happens to us while we are making other plans." There are just so many factors beyond our control. And so when we relentlessly pursue the path of our ego, we do it at the expense of our connection with the Universe. We stop the flow of wisdom, guidance, and inspiration, and we communicate to the Universe that we don't trust it.

Surrender means that you choose to align your actions to serve the highest good of all, which can include making plans all while knowing that you are not in charge of the outcome or timing. You trust that the Universe (or whatever higher power you believe in) will orchestrate everything to ensure it is happening for the highest good of all, which doesn't mean that everything will be easy or rosy. It simply means that you are surrendering your expectations of what you think the outcome, timing, or order of events should be.

Much easier said than done, I know. Especially when it's hard, when it hurts, or when we are in the trenches, it can be hard to trust that everything is working out for our highest good and in Divine timing. The irony is that it is in those times especially that surrendering will allow us to get to the other side faster and with more ease.

You hear about people finding their soul mates when they've stopped looking. I've found this to be true. After a big heartbreak, I'd thought I was done. No more dating for me, at least for the foreseeable future. This disappointment and renunciation ended up creating space for me to process what needed to be released. Without any self-imposed pressure, I could actually be open to whatever came my way with a softness and newfound sense of freedom. I could surrender.

In addition to processing my own feelings as part of my regular spiritual practice, I also decided to do a ThetaHealing, which I had never done before. It is a process of meditation whereby one uses the theta brain wave and focused prayer for healing. I felt as though there were some karmic ties and beliefs that I couldn't quite get to on my own and that I was able to release during this session.

A week later, I met my true soul mate.

Spirit and the Universe work in magical ways, and fast, when we surrender and step aside. My soul mate and I dated long-distance between the US and Germany for a year, during which Spirit arranged everything in Divine timing to allow him to move to the US so we could start to build a life together. This experience has given me a more embodied level of trust that life is working for us, not against us.

Surrender doesn't need to be initiated through heartbreak or other life-altering events, or when our backs are up against a wall. It can be practiced in less intense daily scenarios. Think of a moment when you felt stuck with a task, project, or conversation and decided you needed to take your mind off it for a moment or remove yourself from the situation to clear your head. Maybe you went to the gym, got outside for a walk, took a few deep breaths, or called a dear friend.

Those simple acts of surrendering after realizing that you aren't making headway create space to invite inspiration and guidance. Sure, we always have free will to decide how, when, and why we do things, but when we surrender, we disengage from the struggle of continuing to resist what is best for us. In spiritual surrender, we allow the Divine to show us different ways. We come to see obstacles as detours directing us on a different path. We let go of the concept of failure and stop beating ourselves up to instead let the Divine work through us in new ways with Divine timing.

Spiritual surrender isn't at all passive or submissive, even though a surrendered person may appear that way at times. Being in a state of surrender is being aware of and in tune with the energies at play. The absence of action might simply be intuitive knowing that right now is not the time to act or keep pushing. Spiritual surrender can be quite active, because it requires us to tune in, become aware, actively decide to surrender, and consciously choose the next spirit-aligned action.

The key is healing and letting go of what you expect to occur, how and when you expect it, and who you think you ought to be. Surrendering is not losing the fight or giving up but actually sitting in the fire of spiritual, creative, or personal transformation. This is brave, and it is hard.

As humans with egos, there will always be times when we lose ourselves, and eventually, when the suffering gets too hard, we will remember to surrender. It is in the process of learning how and when to surrender that we learn to trust in not only the laws of the Universe but also our own higher power. We build that trust muscle and a knowing that we have all the tools already inside us to handle what life throws at us.

TRY THIS: PRACTICING SPIRITUAL SURRENDER

Believe me when I say that you will be practicing this for the rest of your life. Just when you thought you surrendered, you will be asked to surrender more. Practice this five-step process to spiritual surrender by Gabby Bernstein, with a few tweaks of my own.

STEP 1: SURRENDER.

Fear or frustration are indicators that you're relying on your own strength and sense of control. The support of the Universe and your guides is always available, but first you must ask for help and then step aside. Ask for support during meditation or prayer; do not try to control for a specific outcome, timing, or process. Allow the Universe to show you what you need and what is for your highest good and the highest good for all. If you struggle asking for support, then start by using this prayer from *A Course in Miracles*:

> Where would you have me go?
> What would you have me do?
> What would you have me say? And to
>   whom?

STEP 2: PRACTICE GRATITUDE.

Instead of focusing on what isn't already apparent in physical manifestation, redirect your focus on what has already manifested. Celebrate all the small and big things in your life and nurture and enjoy this vibration of gratitude, love, and joy.

STEP 3: REFRAME YOUR PERCEPTION OF OBSTACLES OR FAILURE.

Gabby Bernstein suggests recognizing obstacles as detours in the right direction. When one door closes, another door opens—all we have to do is keep walking down the hall until the right door becomes apparent. Think of your current road-block, rejection, or lack of progress as part of the process to redirect you on a path of healing. When we practice spiritual surrender, we can detach from the outcome and trust that what is happening is happening for our highest good.

STEP 4: ASK FOR SIGNS.

Staying in a place of spiritual surrender is hard, and there are going to be times when you catch yourself falling back into old habits and the need to control. You won't always understand why you are being guided down a particular path. That is why it is important to ask for signs. Guidance is all around you, all the time—just pay attention.

STEP 5: WHEN YOU THINK YOU'VE SURRENDERED, SURRENDER MORE!

The ability to surrender is like building strength: it requires practice every day! When we trust and have evidence that we are being supported and guided, then we can afford to be patient and wait without anxiety.

FINDING YOUR INNER VOICE

Once we embrace change, identify when we are distracting ourselves with toxic productivity or other coping mechanisms, and practice surrender, we can learn to find a balance between what "makes sense" and what "feels right," to value both logic and intuition, the language of our soul. We all have that inner voice that speaks to us and guides us. We are all born with the same set of energetic tools to make sense of our inner and outer worlds, to read energy—we literally do it all day long, whether we are aware of it or not. Our intuition never stops communicating; it's just that we stopped listening and developed a tendency to overwrite anything we may perceive through our senses with logic.

While we are all born with the same energetic tools, the way in which intuition communicates to us and how we make sense of it is unique to each and every person, based on how we perceive the world around us.

When you think about it, intuition is really our first language. All of us are born with intuition, and we speak it fluently; babies communicate using their senses before they can speak. It is universal. Children are energetically open, and many have "imaginary friends" that likely aren't imaginary but simply energies adults are no longer receptive to. As we grow older and learn spoken languages as well as how to behave and think, we rely less on our intuition. Thankfully, we simply have to learn to reconnect with it.

Learning the language of intuition means learning to communicate through our feelings. Although intuition is innate, it does take awareness and practice to learn to recognize and trust it. Without awareness and the ability to tap into your emotional body, you will have a hard time recognizing and interpreting intuitive signs. Intuitive signs or pings are often very subtle, but the more we train our intuitive muscle, or *clairs*, quiet our thoughts through meditation, and raise our vibration, the more attuned we become. Think of it like tuning a radio; if you are on the wrong frequency, all you will hear is static, the constant chatter of your thoughts. Once you find that right frequency, however, the noise subsides and you are left with an audible tune, your intuition. Then, just like with any other language, you will need to immerse yourself in it, practice using it in your day-to-day, and learn the subtleties of your own energetic dialect to gain the confidence to use and trust it.

Before I learned how to tap into my intuition, I would give away my power to my parents, my fencing coaches, my teachers, my bosses—basically any person with some sort of authority based on position or age. I let them make decisions for me, because surely they knew best, and I, of course, listened—even if it didn't always feel right. And acting contrary to what they wanted or what I thought they wanted made me anxious and uncomfortable.

That is why it is so important to figure out what you and only you want, foster a trusting relationship with your feeling body, and start practicing following your intuitive guidance on small day-to-day decisions versus jumping into the big, life-altering decisions from the start. That is how you build trust with yourself and give your nervous system a chance to build capacity without overwhelming it, although that still might happen at times.

When dealing with a particular question or decision in my life, I have learned to ask yes-or-no questions and to listen to the response of my body as well as be open to any intuitive downloads from my spirit team. What are my feelings communicating to me? Is the feeling expansive or restrictive? Do I feel a heaviness or a lightness? Do I feel a sense of uneasiness in my gut? What are my paraphysical senses picking up? What are my guides telling me? I've practiced this on decisions like spending money on a trip or course, whether I should go on a date with someone, if I should take on a particular work or personal project, if I should work with a particular teacher. I now know by practicing this what it feels like to me if the answer is yes versus no. Another way to practice using your intuition is to apply intuitive eating principles by feeling what your body needs and craves, how your body wants to move and rest, or even what to wear. You would be surprised at how your intuition can lead you to choosing a particular color that corresponds to a particular energetic vibration you could benefit from.

Quieting the mind and gaining awareness of your emotional body and your feelings is a great first step. And once you start to raise your vibration, you will undoubtedly have an easier time recognizing your intuition as well as intuitive pings from the Universe or your spirit team.

There are many ways in which we can raise our vibration, one of which is meditation. On a daily basis, you can practice gratitude and following the path of the most joy. This helps you stay open and appreciative, as opposed to needy and demanding. A surefire way to access joy is through laughter. We as humans have the innate ability to create a contagious, cathartic, joyous experience at any given moment. Deep belly laughter—like an ecstatic orgasm—can even cause us to transcend space and time. We don't call it having a *sense* of humor for no reason. I believe that the Universe has given us humans a means beyond our five senses to help reduce stress, deal with trying circumstances, and access one of the highest-possible vibrations—the frequency of joy. Laughter and our sense of humor are gifts for our enjoyment, healing, and spiritual transformation. Vibrating at one of the highest frequencies, such as joy, makes it easier to connect with your guides and receive insight, solutions, and opportunities.

. . .

As we become energetically more attuned or sensitive, it is important to practice energetic hygiene in order to remain clear, open, and receptive. Even if you are new to working with energy, clearing and protecting your energy will help you become more sensitive. I was first introduced to the importance of clearing and protecting my energy by my grandmother, and it was later reinforced during my psychic-development classes.

You see, everything is made of energy, and everything has its own unique vibration and energy field, including you, the chair you are sitting on, the flowers at the park. As electromagnetic beings, we carry energy in our energy field, and we attract circumstances and people into our experience that match our frequency and repel anything that doesn't. This is another reason why it is immensely important to become aware of our own frequency, diligently remove anything that does not serve us, and nurture our energy through thoughts, feelings, and actions that are based on high-vibrational frequencies, such as love, joy, and gratitude. Simply speaking, energy vibrates on a frequency spectrum from light to dark or, in other words, from love to fear. The frequency of love feels expansive, abundant, and effortless—it feels like you're in the flow or in alignment. The frequency of fear feels constricting, anxious, and dense.

After learning about this, I started to practice clearing and protecting my energy. I felt nothing. It wasn't that the energy wasn't being cleared or that energy wasn't flowing (it always is), but that I wasn't sensitive enough yet to feel the energy moving. But I kept practicing intuitive awareness by developing my clairs, communicating with Spirit, and clearing and protecting my aura. Today, I can easily tell when I am out of alignment, and I can't imagine not clearing and protecting my energy. Just like I wouldn't go to bed without showering off the dirt of the day, I also won't go to bed without clearing my energy. It is part of my regular "energy hygiene."

TRY THIS: A SIMPLE AND POWERFUL TWO-STEP PROCESS TO CLEAR AND PROTECT

STEP 1: START BY GROUNDING AND CLEARING.

The practice of grounding anchors us into the present moment and brings us back into our bodies. Try the grounding meditation below.

GROUNDING MEDITATION:

- Sit comfortably with your eyes closed and your feet flat on the ground.
- Bring awareness to how you are feeling in this moment, and take a few deep, relaxing breaths.
- Visualize roots growing from your root chakra (at the bottom of your spine) and from the soles of your feet through the ground beneath you, through the dirt, all the way deep to the core of the earth.
- Visualize your roots growing and spreading out— deeply anchoring you to the grounding earth energy.
- Now, visualize a bright star or the moon in the night sky—see a beam of golden-white light connect from this point to your crown chakra (the top of your head). This is the loving, healing, and cleansing source energy.
- Visualize this golden-white light enter through your crown and feel it also wash over you like a warm and comforting shower. Feel this light as it touches your skin, then imagine this light being absorbed by your skin, your muscle tissue, your organs.

- See this light cleanse anything in your body that does not belong to you or no longer serves you. See it wash through you, down through the roots, deep into the earth, where this energy is released and transmuted.
- Then pull this cleansed energy back up through the soles of your feet and base of your spine, up to the center of your heart.
- Connected to Source and anchored to the depths of the earth, breathe into your heart center and bring to mind a few things you are grateful for.
- As you breathe, expand this energy outward, forming an oval-shaped energy field a few feet from your body. Feel this energy encompassing and surrounding you. This is your frequency, your vibration of love and light.

STEP 2: PRACTICE PROTECTING.

Choose any one or a combination of these options below to do once or multiple times a day.

OPTION 1: GOLDEN EGG

- Hold your focus here and relax into this energy space that is yours alone; notice what this feels like when you are unplugged from the collective.
- Now, visualize the outside of your expanded aura hardening with a golden shell—forming a golden egg.
- Affirm to yourself that you are safe and protected within this golden egg and that only energy of light and love can enter your space.

OPTION 2: SHOWER PRACTICE (SUPER EASY TO
INCORPORATE INTO YOUR DAILY ROUTINE!)

- Imagine the water that is falling over your head
  and your body to be a warm golden-white light.
- Visualize this light shower clearing your aura
  of anything that is not yours or no longer serving you.
- In your mind's eye, see any "gunk" be washed
  down the drain.
- As you are drying off, visualize the outside of your
  cleared aura harden with a golden shell—forming
  a golden egg.
- Affirm to yourself that you are safe and protected
  within this golden egg and that only energy of
  light and love can enter your space.

OPTION 3: PRAYER OF PROTECTION

Divine Parent,
I ask that you surround me with white
light of healing, love, and protection.

Help me disconnect from the collective energies so I may focus on connecting
to my own higher self.

And raise my vibrations so that I may
connect with Source and my spirit loved
ones during this time.

I ask my spirit loved ones, guides, and
light beings to step forward to provide me
with messages of healing, love, guidance, and
support in ways that I can easily perceive.

May the guidance be clear, and may I
have the awareness to recognize it.
And so it is.

EVERYONE IS PSYCHIC: THE FIVE CLAIRS

Ever since I've been more public about the fact that I am a psychic medium/intuitive, skeptics enjoy challenging me. "How do you know where the information comes from?" they ask. "How can I know that the information I receive is from Spirit?" And: "Where is the evidence?"

It is in no way my job to convince anyone or prove anything. My only job is to try to show up as authentically as possible and to further deepen the trust I have to follow my fierce feminine intuition, to remove the mystery and misperceptions around psychic/energetic gifts, and to help others do the same.

I have started to answer these questions with my own set of questions: Do you believe that creativity exists? Where does creativity come from? Can you prove where it comes from? My point in posing these questions is not to be a smart-ass (well, maybe a little) but rather to get people to think about certain abilities (like creativity) that we accept as normal and both innate and trainable without being able to fully explain them.

So where does creativity come from? How do you receive your creative vision, a melody, a beat or riff? What inspires you?

Many artists, when asked about their source of inspiration, say that they had a vision or a dream, that they saw or heard something that caught their attention. Many artists would even say that their talents are God-given or sacred gifts. I agree! Inspiration equals "in Spirit." Many artists have rituals around accessing their creative state or flow—a sort of meditative and receptive state. Artists allow inspiration to flow through them as a channel and then manifest in the form of their craft. Inspiration is a catalyst to allow imagination and creative juices to flow and bring visions, feelings, and audible experiences to life.

As a society, we accept that artists are inspired, imaginative, and sometimes even a little "out there" with their creative and personal expression. It is deemed totally "normal." Art and creative energy are widely celebrated socially and culturally—and rightfully so.

I've never heard anyone deny that creativity, imagination, and inspiration exist. Although some people might be more creatively inclined or talented, everyone has the ability to cultivate their creativity. After all, this is the function of our right-brain hemisphere, which is associated with creativity, imagination, intuition, insight, visualization, and holistic thought.

Now, the aha moment you've all been waiting for . . . intuitives and psychic mediums use the same right-brain hemisphere to process inspiration, intuition, and energy and to express this through their craft—most often in the form of spoken and written words. Intuitives receive energy, read and decipher it, and use it to inspire, heal, and create messages.

Can you see where I am going with this?

If we can agree that inspiration, creativity, and intuition are functions of our right-brain hemisphere and that all human beings have access to these functions, then all of us have the ability to feel, hear, see, and perceive inspiration.

Everyone is psychic!

Oh yes, I said it. Cue the gasps, the shocked faces, the disbelief, and the denial. You don't need to believe it for it to be true. People used to believe that the world was flat (some still do), but the truth has always been that it is round.

Just as we tap into our creativity, we tap into our psychic abilities all the time—even if subconsciously. By allowing expression from the Universe, psychics and mediums challenge the notion that any inspired information from "outside" of us has to be from God as defined by Judeo-Christian dogma. And therefore the word *psychic* has been categorized as witchcraft. Not as we witches define witchcraft, of course, but within the scary, narrow, negative definition used by society at large.

Would you call creativity witchcraft?

As human beings, we all have the same fleshy vessel outfitted with the same receptive tools to receive energetic inputs. Some pray, some create rituals, some dance, and some meditate to access the inner world and allow inspiration to occur. While not everyone is an artist, everyone has creative ability. While not everyone is a psychic medium, everyone has psychic ability. Even Albert Einstein, a physicist who spent his life analyzing and proving hypotheses, understood that there is more at work than can be proved through logic. Einstein is often credited with calling the intuitive mind a sacred gift and the rational mind a faithful servant.

Part of connecting and developing our intuitive/psychic gifts can be learning to tap into our five paraphysical senses. Most of us are in tune with our physical senses of touch, taste, smell, sight, and hearing. But we also have senses that detect energy that lies outside of what we are able to perceive through just our physical senses; those are part of what is called our paraphysical sensory system, or clairs. *Clair* comes from French and means "clear"; clairs are our clear senses that are able to work with invisible stimuli to help provide us with clarity.

For example, recall that feeling when you walk into a room and sense the tension. Of course, you are using your physical senses, like sight, to assess the situation, but the tension or energy is perceived through your paraphysical sense of *clairsentience*. Or that song that keeps popping into your head: you hear it with your paraphysical sense of *clairaudience* even though it isn't playing audibly out in the world. When the song

"Sing" by Shirley Bassey comes to mind, I am transported to lying in bed and singing this song with my grandmother. I feel joyful, secure, and connected to her. This is the particular experience and association I have with this song and my grandmother, and, in those moments, I know that she is with me.

THE FIVE CLAIRS:

* *Clairvoyance*: clear seeing. Think of it as images or visions being projected right onto the mind's eye. These are images that bypass the visual system, so this can happen with eyes open or closed.
* *Clairaudience*: clear hearing. This is the ability to hear voices or sounds inside your head that usually appear out of nowhere. You can think of it as the way you hear in your dreams.
* *Clairsentience/claircognizance*: clear sensing. Many empaths would be considered clairsentient. Think of it as being able to feel other people's feelings or to know certain information.
* *Clairgustance*: clear tasting. This is the ability to perceive taste without having anything in your mouth. Think of it like being able to taste and smell your grandmother's pie by just thinking of it.
* *Clairalience*: clear smelling. This is the ability to perceive aroma, fragrance, or odor. As your olfactory system is closely linked to memory, the psychic impression often has to do with a memory that contains a message.

Most of us have one or two clairs that are naturally more developed and come more easily to us. My primary clairs are clairvoyance and clairsentience, although I sometimes

51

receive messages through claircognizance and clairaudience. However, we all have the ability to develop all five clairs over time.

TRY THIS: DEVELOPING YOUR CLAIRS

The first thing to do is establish a regular meditation practice to quiet the outside world and limit the stimuli that keep you tuned in to your physical sensory system. If you don't have a regular practice yet, start with five minutes per day and work yourself up to a minimum of twenty minutes, at least three times per week. (See also my Beginner's Guide to Meditation on www.siobhanclaire.com/blog.)

Below are a few fun and easy exercises to help you practice your clairs.

CLAIRVOYANCE:

- Practice visualization: for ten to fifteen minutes each day, imagine your dream home/job/relationship like a movie with as much detail as possible (colors, feelings, textures, etc.). This is a good way to practice clairvoyance as well as manifestation.
- Practice seeing images: have a friend give you an image and describe in detail what you see, including colors, textures, and any other sensations that come up.
- Isolate clairvoyance: if you already use your clairs to receive messages or give readings, practice solely using your clairvoyance without any other impressions from the other clairs.

CLAIRAUDIENCE:

- Listen: practice listening to subtle sounds; instead of tuning out sounds, allow them to come in.
- Isolate clairaudience: practice solely using your clairaudience without any other impressions from the other clairs. Ask your guides to help you with clairaudience by giving you a name or a street sign in your readings.

CLAIRSENTIENCE, OR CLAIRCOGNIZANCE:

- Practice psychometry: tune in to the energy of an object by touching it with your hands. Try to pick up a feeling for a person, place, or thing.
- Practice feeling: have someone hide an object in your home and try to feel where the object is. Imagine a beam of light connecting you to the energy of the item and ask yourself questions such as *"Does this feel high or low? Is it covered?"* Then listen to how your body responds.

CLAIRGUSTANCE AND CLAIRALIENCE:

- Tasting and smelling: ask a partner or friend to eat something—a piece of chocolate, fruit, bread, etc.—without telling you what they are eating. Try to sense what they are eating by tuning in to their energy. Ask yourself: "Is it sweet, savory, or sour? What does it smell like? Is it soft or crunchy?"

Remember that there is no wrong way to do this, as everyone gets different input to their clairs, and therefore the experience is very individualized. Just like everyone perceives the world through their own filter, the same is true about how you receive intuitive/psychic impressions. The most important thing is to trust what comes and to have the courage to express and act on it.

REFLECTION

- Have you had experiences that forced or propelled you to leap into the unknown? Did you choose that leap for yourself? Or were you following others' expectations?
- Were there moments leading up to these experiences when you ignored your intuition?
- How did you feel about the experiences? How did you cope with the emotions at the time?
- What are the consequences of these experiences that you are living today?
- When did you start silencing your voice and ignoring your own needs?
- How did silencing your voice and neglecting your own needs make you feel about these life experiences?
- Can you pay attention to your feelings? Do you stop and take the time to drop into your feelings, or do you automatically look to your mind to tell you what you are experiencing and what your response should be? What are you doing to build a relationship with your feelings and your body?
- What is the feeling in your body when you are faced with change? Do you feel you can relax into it, trusting your inner guidance system? Or do you resist and try to control due to fear of the unknown?

- In what ways could you practice surrendering in your daily life?
- Have you experienced tapping into the paraphysical sensory system? Do you feel an affinity with any of the five clairs (clairvoyance, clairaudience, clairsentience/claircognizance, clairgustance, clairalience)?

CHAPTER 3

YOUR EVOLUTION ISN'T ALWAYS GOING TO BE PRETTY

There I was again, four years later, traveling to Istanbul to take my second shot at qualifying for the Olympics. This time was different. I had my coach with me as well as representation from the Irish Fencing Federation. I had the support of my teammates back at the Ohio State University. Most importantly, I had experience with being at an Olympic qualifier event. This time around only the top two fencers would qualify.

Like last time, I had fought my way to the semifinals. But now, I had to win. It was a head-to-head, touch-by-touch fight until the score was 14–14. The next person to score would secure their spot at the 2008 Olympics. Seventeen years of work toward my Olympic dream came down to a few seconds and one single touch.

I vividly remember talking to myself in that moment as I was getting ready to step onto the *en garde* line. I clearly evoked the memory and the feeling that I'd had four years prior when I'd lost: the feeling of defeat, of burnout, like everything I'd worked for had been for nothing. It was now or never. "C'mon, Siobhan," I said to myself. "Fucking do it. This time it's your turn. You've worked too hard and given up too much. Do not let her take this from you. You just have to fucking do it." I could feel the adrenaline pumping through my veins and the determination growing. I was laser-focused on getting that one last touch. There was no way in hell I was going to feel that way again.

So I fought as hard as I've ever fought. I put every ounce of energy, every drop of blood, sweat, and tears into it. And when my final touch lit up the scoreboard, I fell to my knees, unleashing a guttural scream from deep within. It wasn't even happiness; it was simply a release. After everything, I'd done it. I had qualified for the Olympic Games.

I didn't take a moment to sit back and revel in my victory. Instead, I jumped straight into the pressure cooker, rising to a very different level of stress from the kind I'd previously encountered, one that few ever do. All of a sudden, I wasn't trying to please just the usual suspects—my coach, my parents, my team, my school, myself—but the entire world.

I immediately set off on a whirlwind pre-Olympic tour, traveling to Ireland and Germany to give interviews with the press and returning to the Ohio State University in Columbus to do the same. My Irish family was planning a watch party in the middle of the night, and friends and family were traveling all the way to China to watch me compete. My father expressed his discomfort about me getting all this attention in Ireland, which I interpreted as him being worried that I would embarrass him. Though everyone was supportive and proud in their own way, I felt it as another weight on top of me. My ego, my fear, started to run away with me, muddying my perception and robbing me of joy or even basic satisfaction in my accomplishment. More than anything, I worried that I would disappoint.

On August 9, 2008—four days before my twenty-fourth birthday—I was in the prep area, where eight of us fencers were waiting to step into the arena for the first time. It was tense and quiet, everyone preparing themselves—shaking out arms and legs, jumping up and down to stay warm, checking equipment; some had headphones on, while others were talking with their coaches. I was nervously shifting my weight from one leg to the other, feeling overwhelmed and stuck in my head. "This is it," I told myself. "This is the moment you have worked for all your life. You can do it."

We entered the arena. Each pairing of two fencers and their coaches followed the umpire to their assigned *piste*. There were four *pistes* laid out in a quadrant, each with a color: blue, yellow, red, and green. I was on the blue *piste*. The stands were filled with hundreds of cheering spectators, which is very unusual for fencing, and there were huge electronic scoreboards and screens to show the fencing action in close-up and slow motion. The tension on the floor was so thick you could cut it with a saber. I stepped onto the *piste* in my "shiny armor," ready to perfectly please my coach, my family, and my country.

"*En garde!*" said the umpire.

We stepped onto the start line.

"*Pret!*"

We took our position.

"*Allez!*"

My mind went blank.

It was as if I wasn't even present, and the harder I tried to focus, the more my fear of losing took hold of me. I was completely disembodied, and my mind was fogged by fear of failure. My opponent from Poland easily ran away with the first few touches. My fear of failure turned into panic with every touch as I got closer to losing the bout. At the break I was down 8–1. I had a chance to breathe and refocus and realize that I really had nothing left to lose. In the second half of the bout, I was back in the game, and we went head-to-head, taking turns scoring, but it wasn't enough. One minute and thirty-two seconds later, my Olympic dream was over. The score was 15–8. Still in a daze, I stepped off the *piste*. I was heartbroken and humiliated. My biggest fear of letting everyone down had become my reality. My perfect facade crumbled all around me.

Afterward, the people closest to me said strange and hurtful things to me: "What kind of performance was that?" "You shouldn't have been there in the first place." "There is an obvious difference between college fencing and world-class fencing."

These words were no less cruel than what I was saying to myself: "Did you really think you could do well?" "You're a joke; how embarrassing." "You're a worthless piece of shit!" I oscillated between hating myself and feeling sorry for myself. What I really needed was a hug, maybe even to hear "I am proud of you" or "This is really hard, and I am here for you when you're ready" or "I know you're heartbroken, and that's OK." Or even someone holding space for me and my emotional roller coaster would have been enough—no words needed. But no one did, not in the way I needed it, nor could I give that to myself.

And so I hit rock bottom. I felt less than worthless, like I was the world's greatest disappointment, like all my hopes and dreams and years invested had been a waste of time. I was beaten down and hurting worse than I've ever hurt in my life. I immediately moved into numbing survival mode and threw a little self-sabotage into the mix, because why not? Drinking, partying, casual sex, anything to numb the pain and escape reality for a minute or two.

I also isolated myself from the "outside world," avoiding

conversations with anyone from the Irish delegation, my family, my coach, or my teammates, and immersed myself in the microcosm that is the Olympics. My event was the first event on the first day of the Olympics, so I got to spend the remaining two weeks in the Olympic Village, watching other Olympic events, and attending parties that were only for Olympians. Sounds like a dream, right? Certainly, this was a once-in-a-lifetime experience. It was a lot of fun and probably doesn't sound like rock bottom—I get it. But things aren't always what they seem. I felt lost, alone with the pain and a deep self-hatred. As Michael Phelps says in the HBO documentary *The Weight of Gold*: "A good 80 percent, maybe more, go through some sort of post-Olympic depression." Once the doors to the Olympic Village close, we are left alone to figure out how to piece our lives, identities, and mental states back together. Coupled with the tendency for athletes to not talk about feelings or weaknesses, we suffer in silence. And in too many cases it ends in suicide.

I'm not saying that there is anything inherently wrong with partying, drinking, and casual sex. The problem was that I was using them to avoid feeling, which is fine in the short term but doesn't address the underlying issues or solve anything. It was as though I was sending a big *fuck you* to always trying to do the right thing, to performing, to meeting other people's expectations, to being perfect. I'd tried, hadn't I? And I'd failed, and hard, in front of the entire world, at the event I'd spent my entire life preparing for. After all that, what was the point?

DARK NIGHT OF THE SOUL

I wish someone would have told me about the *dark night of the soul*. Because there I was, in the middle of it, hurting like I'd never hurt before, not sure about anything, not sure if I had the wherewithal or even the desire to put one foot in front of the other.

Of course, knowing about it wouldn't have prevented me from having to go through it. But it would have let me know that these periods of intense emotional clearing eventually end and leave us with new knowledge, clarity, or energetic sensibilities.

Competing on the Olympic stage did not at all turn out the way I had hoped or expected. This experience became a tipping point in my healing journey. It took me years to come to terms with the resulting emotions, to cope with personal relationships that had changed, and to deal with how I saw myself. My tipping point might have been on the world's largest stage, but the emotional turmoil I experienced is transferable.

I believe that it is important to shed light on how spiritual awakenings can manifest in order to normalize what we feel in the process of letting go of that which no longer serves us. Everyone understands that traumatic life experiences are hard and can evoke a lot of emotions. And while this can trigger a spiritual awakening, it is not the only way. Sometimes emotional wounds aren't related to a certain identifiable moment, action, or situation, which can leave us confused, especially when it seems like our feelings don't match the circumstances. Quite often we are processing deep-seated and even karmic baggage. We might undergo a period of debilitating grief and might not immediately understand why. We might have an extreme feeling of shame or guilt and won't immediately be able to place it. Maybe we have unprocessed anger that we project onto others who don't deserve our wrath. The focus of many modern spiritual teachings is often centered on alignment, peace, awareness, consciousness, and bliss, but they don't always come with a disclaimer such as: "Beware! Might cause you to experience a dark night of the soul."

A spiritual awakening in conjunction with a dark night of the soul is a natural process of your soul evolving, a time to confront your shadow in a very raw and primal way to allow for a more conscious expansion. As someone on the path, as a Woman in Total Conscious Healing, you will likely have more than one.

From where I stand today, I can recall catalysts for a spiritual awakening or expanding energetically, but I wasn't always ready to do the deep work required to face my shadow. My post-Olympics flailing was one such moment—I simply had no clue what it even meant to go deep, nor did I have the tools to support myself.

And so I carried on and did what I do: I stuffed my feelings down, down, down, and went to work. I had two months to finalize my graduate-school applications and study for the GRE and the GMAT. I also had to find a place to stay and a job so I could pay the bills—I had graduated, so the scholarship funds had run dry. I started working at the Ohio State Wexner Medical Center as a part-time outpatient coder. I also continued practicing and took on an informal assistant-coaching position while I waited to see if I got accepted into grad school. I knew that in order to continue competing on the World Cup circuit and to try for a third Olympics, I would need to commit to training full-time. But I couldn't even think about making that decision; I was still hurting. All the struggles had made me lose my passion for the sport. My heart was no longer in it. I also didn't have the funds. So when I got accepted to graduate school and was awarded a graduate assistant position working part-time for one of the hospital executives, I decided to hang up my saber and my mask for good. I never picked it back up.

After I earned my master's degree in health administration from the Ohio State University, I moved to New York City and got my first corporate job at Ernst & Young. I buckled down, put my nose to the grindstone.

What I would eventually learn years later is that we often create or prolong our own suffering by trying to contain our feelings, by shutting off our capacity to feel altogether. We numb out and then overcompensate, getting dopamine hits by succumbing to whatever coping mechanism we are used to (busyness, achievements, sugar, alcohol, drugs, chaos, drama, sex, shopping, porn, etc.). These coping behaviors then often pile on another layer of shame and guilt, because we know deep down inside that we are harming ourselves, emotionally and physically. It took me many years to work toward forgiveness of myself and others, to understand that our behaviors are directly correlated with our level of conscious awareness and emotional maturity. I realized that I had responded by suppressing and numbing. This was the only way I knew how to cope at the time. Luckily, I survived.

It wasn't until the summer of 2019, however, after a fleeting encounter with a karmic soul mate, that I was consciously aware of being in a dark night of the soul. By then, I'd been on my spiritual journey for a while, and I'd laid the groundwork—I was ready to shed some layers. He and I had quickly learned that we had some fundamental and irreconcilable differences in our belief systems. He was a devout Christian looking for a devout Christian wife; I was a psychic who'd long ago shed the Catholicism of my youth and was looking for a partner with whom I could further explore and expand consciousness. He believed in a singular Christian god; I did not. He was happy with the patriarchal structures of traditional Christianity; I was not. Yet we were deeply attracted to each other and surprised by the intensity of our soul connection. On only our second date, while watching the sunset in Riverside Park on the west side of Manhattan, we had to talk about how strange this feeling of "recognition" was between us.

"What do you think it is?" he asked.

"We recognize each other from previous lives," I answered simply.

He looked at me like I was nuts. After a moment, he recited the poem "To a Stranger" by Walt Whitman:

> Passing stranger! you do not know how
>   longingly I look upon you,
> You must be he I was seeking, or she I
>   was seeking, (it comes to me as of a
>   dream,)
> I have somewhere surely lived a life of joy
>   with you,
> All is recall'd as we flit by each other, fluid,
>   affectionate, chaste, matured,
> You grew up with me, were a boy with me
>   or a girl with me,
> I ate with you and slept with you, your
>   body has become not yours only nor
>   left my body mine only,
> You give me the pleasure of your eyes,
>   face, flesh, as we pass, you take of my
>   beard, breast, hands, in return,
> I am not to speak to you, I am to think of
>   you when I sit alone or wake at night
>   alone,
> I am to wait, I do not doubt I am to meet
>   you again,
> I am to see to it that I do not lose you.

Exactly, I thought. *He gets it.*

Still, no matter how we tried to turn it, there was no way for us to be together, and after an extraordinary two-week romance, we decided to not see each other again. It made sense, of course, but our hearts don't understand sense.

Once I let sink in what had transpired and what I had recognized and felt at a soul level, I fell into a deep period of depression. I felt as if I were grieving a death, the type of pain that comes from deep down in your belly and knocks you off your feet. I sobbed until I could hardly catch my breath. I felt crazy. My intense emotional response was disproportionate to the situation—logically speaking. How could a passing stranger cause this much emotional upheaval? What I was experiencing was obviously much bigger than this two-week romance, and it wasn't all about him either.

I was confused, and I felt alone in the process, as though nobody could relate to what I was going through, and I couldn't really explain it either—I hadn't gotten there yet. All I knew was that the pain kept coming in waves that nearly swept me away. I desperately tried to stuff down all the emotions like I used to, but I couldn't. I just wanted to disconnect, to step away from everyone and everything.

I remember, a few months after this person and I called it quits, I was working late in a hotel room in downtown Minneapolis, where I was for a work trip, and I couldn't stop the tears from running down my cheeks. I put my work away—clearly, there would be no more productivity that night. Lying in the big, comfy hotel bed and scrolling through social media, I came across a blog post describing a "dark night of the soul" as the realization that much of what we are taught in society and by its structures doesn't make sense anymore, leading us to question what life is about. We start to gain awareness of the roles we play to gain approval and to be loved. What resonated with me the most was the description of feeling tired, isolated, and disconnected while also having a deep desire to be alone. We feel misunderstood while simultaneously grieving our old selves and our old views of the world. We crave direction, meaning, and purpose in our lives.

There they were: the words to describe what I was going through. I felt seen, understood, and less crazy. I felt relieved.

All the little intuitive hits, feelings, and thoughts clicked together like puzzle pieces. I understood that that brief romance had been a karmic encounter to evoke a dark night of the soul.

This time I was ready for it, for this much-needed energetic release and upgrade. Knowing what I had signed up for and that what I was feeling and going through was par for the course made it so much easier for me to allow it.

TRY THIS: LETTER TO SELF

Use this exercise to clear your past, forgive yourself and others, appreciate the lessons, and open your heart to yourself and others. Write a letter to your past self or your past lovers/friends/family. (You don't need to send it, but more power to you if you do.)

I wrote this letter to myself as I was going through this dark night of the soul:

> Dear One,
> I am sorry I did not know how to hold your heart.
>
> I am sorry I hurt you and that I did not respect your boundaries.
>
> I am sorry I ignored your needs and allowed others to dictate your worth.
>
> I am asking for forgiveness for the parts I played in your sadness, pain, doubt, and grief.
>
> But I also am inviting you to recognize your ability to feel the depths of your

shadow, which mirrors your ability to
love.

I thank you for your bravery and
courage in wading through the depths and
working so hard to keep your heart open.

Thank you for being on this path of
true expansion and transformation, no
matter how messy it gets and how misunderstood you might feel at times.

I promise it is worth it. You are right
where you need to be.
—Self

YOUR SPIRIT GUIDES

One afternoon during my dark night of the soul, I went for a
walk in Central Park to clear my head. It was August 4, 2019.
At the Conservatory Garden, I sat down on a concrete wall to
take in the beautiful flower display. "Please," I asked my guides,
"give me a sign that I am on the right path, that things will get
easier."

A monarch butterfly, a sign I recognized, landed next to
me. As I looked closer, I saw that it had settled on the words *Te
Amo* carved in the concrete.

Isn't it nice to know that we are not alone? That we don't
have to rely on our own strength to make it through difficult
times? Each of us has our own spirit guides that we can call
on to navigate our spiritual growth. They communicate with
us in a variety of ways by arranging synchronicities or signs,
enhancing our intuition, intensifying encounters with others,
offering healing, and helping us move toward joy.

It is my belief that, before we reincarnate into our current lifetime, we decide what we need to learn to advance our soul's growth. Based on that, we choose spirit guides who can assist us and benefit from this energetic expansion. This is a mutually agreed-upon relationship, a match to our energetic vibration and our mutual project of growth.

Spirit guides are not bound by space and time the way we are. Some guides are with us throughout our lives, or even lifetimes, while others join or exit our paths at particular junctions. They do not interfere with our free will; they might try to steer and influence, but they will never intervene unless you invite them to.

The Universe, Spirit, or guides only give us what we can handle or what we need to know. Asking for information on exactly how your entire life will unfold wouldn't be helpful. We learn by being in the trenches, during the good and the bad, having our experiences and our feelings. Guides will support us in finding the path of least resistance and the most joy, but we need to be willing to give up our control, to surrender, to trust, and to receive.

TYPES OF GUIDES:

- Light beings, master guides, and angels: Referred to as *light beings* because they are usually perceived as pure light. They often help those whose lifework involves higher planes or higher frequencies, such as healers and spiritual teachers. Master guides and angels aren't bound by space and time and therefore can help or guide many beings at the same time.
- Archetypal guides: Often a Native American medicine (wo)man or shaman, a monk or a nun, a priestess, a warrior, or a healer, these guides present in ways that have a symbolic meaning. They

reactivate soul memory of identities and characteristics from previous lives that can be of help in this lifetime.

• Ancestral guides: These guides knew us through our physical lineage in this lifetime. Often in the form of a grandparent or other relative, they are considered helpers or spirit loved ones. They show up to support us and provide us healing and comfort.

• Animal guides: Spirit animals, or totems, are common in shamanism. Like archetypal guides, spirit animals represent characteristics and energies that have a symbolic meaning to us, our lives, or our current situation.

• Your higher self: Undoubtedly the most important guide of all. The higher self contains our eternal soul energy and our soul's knowledge and wisdom, projected through our physical body. It contains everything learned from our countless prior lives.

TRY THIS: CONNECTING WITH YOUR GUIDES

How do we experience or become aware of our spirit guides and their guidance? We get quiet, pay attention, and listen. This sounds simple, and it can be just that, but it becomes easier when we raise our own vibration and increase our intuitive awareness.

STEP 1: SET AN INTENTION.

As with almost all spiritual work, your intention is important. Thought creates energy that affects consciousness. Having pure intentions, seeking guidance for your highest good and the highest good of all, is therefore essential.

> *I am a clear and honest channel, and it is my intent to not let my opinions, beliefs, and perceptions interfere with messages from Spirit.*

> *I am guided and supported, always.*

> *I intend to keep my heart open when things get hard.*

STEP 2: MEET YOUR GUIDES.

With practice you can become familiar with the feeling of your guides' presence. Meet your guides using guided meditations, such as one of mine on Insight Timer: "Meet Your Spirit Team."

During meditation, you can also ask your guides to identify themselves to you in order of importance, and then listen—you might get a name (although this isn't common in the beginning) or a sensation. Don't overthink it. Memorize this sensation; ask them to take it away and then bring it back to reassure you that you are not simply imagining it. You can then ask the guides to switch and see if you get another sensation or name.

STEP 3: BUILD A RELATIONSHIP.

Instead of waiting to connect with your guides until you have a problem, get into the habit of asking and receiving often. A few examples follow:

- "Dear Spirit/guides/angels, I am surrendering my fear/frustration around _____ to you. I know that I am being guided and that I do not have to solve this on my own. I ask for your support and guidance in a way that I can clearly perceive. I am open to being guided to creative solutions and opportunities that are beyond my own physical perception. Thank you."

• "Thank you, guides of the highest good, for leading me to solutions for my issue/problem/struggle with _____."

• "Thank you, guides, for showing me that which I need to know to move in the direction of love and joy."

• Simply ask for a sign and then pay attention. You can get very specific and ask them to show you a particular symbol or animal or ask to hear a particular song. Stay open and curious.

STEP 4: LISTEN AND WITNESS.

Guides communicate their messages to us in ways that we can perceive and understand. Pay attention to your thoughts and feelings in those moments. Do you get chills, or feel a drop in your gut, an aha moment, relief? For example, we might receive communication through:

• Intuitive pings via psychic clairs. You might have an inner knowing, feel or sense guidance, hear a voice, or have a strong intuition or realization.

• Electrical interference, including sparks of light, glitches on your phone screen, flickering lamps, etc.

• Books falling off shelves or opening to a specific page, a specific oracle card falling out of the deck, a billboard or a social media post or message that resonates.

71

STEP 5: TRY AUTOMATIC WRITING.

If you are looking for answers to specific questions and having difficulty receiving answers through your clairs or during meditations, then try automatic writing. After meditating, set a clear intention. You can write down an invitation to your guides to help you, then ask them to introduce themselves through a sensation or a name. Write down your question and take a moment to visualize energy flowing from Source through your crown, down through your hand and into the pen. Then, without judgment or expectation, write what you feel or perceive. If you are overanalyzing or trying to rationalize, then switch to your nondominant hand. Channeled messages are apparent when the answers are written in a different tone from your own, in a different handwriting, or in second person.

GRIEF AND COMPASSION

Once we choose the spiritual path of awakening and have gotten a glimpse of who we are underneath all the layers of armor, there is no turning back. The more conscious we become, the harder it will be to stay in our comfort zones because we will recognize when we are hiding, playing small, or simply resisting what is.

Whatever the circumstances are that cause you to awaken, your awakening comes with all kinds of emotions, and you can be certain that will include a layer of grief. In some ways, you could say that the spiritual path and the path of a W.I.T.C.H. are ones of loss, as you will lose everything that isn't who you are at your core or isn't for the benefit of the greater good.

Often, this grief is caused by the painful realization that you are losing the version of yourself that you have always known. You are grieving connections that were based on that old version of yourself. It is a painful realization; it can feel like your life is a lie and you don't know where you belong. It can feel like death. In fact, some call such an awakening the death of your ego, or ego death.

Grief is an integral part of any awakening, and that is why it is important to learn to embody it. If we don't, then our ego will continue to tell stories and pull us back into our conditioning, back into our fearful, chaotic thoughts. Even the emotion of grief might be more comfortable than the alternative, as it continues to connect us to our old self, our former life. Allowing grief to move through us and to transmute can feel scary, like a betrayal, which is why many of us would rather stay with what is familiar, even if it is painful.

But we cannot heal if we can't let go of our ego story and conditioning. We can certainly examine the situation to better understand our role in it and its purpose in our trajectory, but be aware of how the mind likes to create and cling to stories that serve the ego. Questions like "Why didn't he choose me?" or "Why is this happening to me?" have just as much potential to be illuminating as they do to be defensive or self-aggrandizing. By trying to figure out what should or shouldn't be, we run the risk of putting ourselves in conflict with what is and who we are becoming. The fact is, we won't always know why something is happening, or what the purpose is, or even what the lesson, or silver lining, will be. And sometimes things just won't make sense in the moment, which is where we end up having no other choice but to surrender.

As we surrender to the different phases of grief, it is also important to get an understanding of who we are in the present moment, what it is that we are feeling, and what it is our heart needs. This is how we learn to embody our emotions and actively allow them. We might scream, ugly-cry, punch a pillow, meditate, or get a massage. By having a greater understanding of our true self and our needs, we can allow space for what is emerging for us and within us throughout all of what life has in store for us—the good and the bad.

Grief can be both very painful and beautiful, because it almost always comes with a tremendous amount of love. You can't mourn something without loving it first—the depth of our grief is evidence of our capacity to feel love.

So when you are faced with grief in your spiritual awakening, remember that and try to make friends with it. Grief, just like any other emotion, will take up space regardless, so why not let it flow through you so you can open your heart to more love, to new possibilities and a new you—in true W.I.T.C.H. fashion.

Once I'd discovered the concept of the dark night of the soul, I let myself grieve, or, rather, I relinquished my futile efforts to control and admitted that I had no choice but to be in it and to let it take its course.

I'll say it again: it hurt. It was messy, dark, and lonely. I was more than a little uncomfortable. I screamed and ugly-cried and punched pillows and drank lots of hot tea and wrapped myself in blankets.

My pain led me to do the deeper soul work, and I was guided to teachings and teachers who were honest and transparent about the shadow work that is necessary, who walked the talk and had gone through their own dark nights and arrived on the other side with a unique capacity to hold space for others.

Eventually, after about six months, the grief subsided.

What I was left with was a softening of my entire being. Some of the armor that I had built to be safe in this patriarchal world fell away. In order to get through my dark night of the soul, I had to show myself a lot of compassion, to consciously allow myself to fall apart, and to allow my feelings to just be there. I chose to come out of the spiritual closet. I chose to clear and work through karmic gunk that remained in this lifetime, and I did a ThetaHealing to address karmic ties. I had to hold myself and lean on my coven to hold space for me, to rely on my spiritual practice. This is exactly why we create a spiritual practice—not for the easy days when everything is flowing, but for the tough days when we need a little extra help finding a way back to ourselves.

I softened so much that people who hadn't seen me in a while noticed. A beautiful soul came up to me after an in-person séance to tell me that she hardly recognized me because my energy was so much softer and not as harsh as before. How lovely to be seen in my new skin.

As the saying goes, "When the student is ready, the teacher will appear." I needed this magical, destabilizing romantic encounter to stir me up and bring an unexamined shadow to the surface. This was the catalyst for an awakening and for coming home to myself.

TOOLS FOR THE TRIAL

The beauty of signing up to do the work is knowing that we will be given opportunities for growth and expansion, but never more than what we can handle. Every dark night of the soul serves a purpose and adds a new tool to your life tool kit, something you can use when the next dark night arrives. You don't have to wait for those extreme energetic upgrades, however—you'll use your tools for every small trial you undergo to decondition, to heal wounds, to integrate lessons, to surrender, and to create a deeper spiritual connection. Everything you go through in this lifetime as a W.I.T.C.H. and everything you learn along the way is preparing you for what is to come. Every class and ritual, every dark night and new dawn, is part of a whole.

My newfound softness was an invitation to explore my emotional body further and to invite in new levels of intimacy in relationships. My emotions were no longer the enemy, a distraction from the real task at hand, a weakness. It felt as if I were being released from an emotional and mental prison. Crying, screaming, squealing, hissing, scowling, laughing. Dancing, punching, gyrating. I started to embody and to express, to use my breath more purposefully, to unclench and unstick. These are tools I use almost daily. I dance to shake off frustration. I allow my tears to flow shamelessly. I growl when I am frustrated. I squeal in a high-pitched tone when I am excited. I become aware when I am holding back, tensing up, clenching my jaw. I breathe and let go, learning to not hold back any longer, to not suffer in silence any longer. To be seen and loved with my ugly, dark, vulnerable, giddy expressions, has been a very great challenge that has brought me to my edge, but I've learned that my vulnerable feminine expression can be met by the mature masculine energy, and I can feel heard and safe.

I've witnessed a friend endure a terrible breakup, go through a yearlong dark night of the soul, find a new partner, quit her job, and sell her house—she resurfaced having found herself, her identity, and her power, all of which she had lost in her previous relationship. Others in my coven have taken their dark nights of the soul, terrible losses, and bouts of grief, and turned those lessons into books, courses, and ceremonies—realizing their newfound tools aren't just for them but for the greater good. Others have rediscovered passions, changed their looks, come out of the closet, switched jobs, gone back to school. The lessons and revelations we have during our dark nights of the soul are so varied, but, regardless of how difficult it is to be in it, you will come out the other end with newfound direction, clarity, strength, personal power, confidence, softness, vulnerability, purpose, passion, love, and compassion—with newfound tools.

It is one thing to go through our own period of awakening and to use our tools to anchor ourselves, but how do we cope when we are the support system for someone else? How do we apply our tools and gifts to be of service and to make this world a better place for all beings? It is much easier (although not always easy) to be in a spiritually aligned place when everything in our lives is in order and we only need to focus on ourselves. Although it is much harder to rely on our spiritual practice when chaos or disruption happens, that is when it is the most important. We simply don't grow and awaken in our comfort zones. And we all know that personal relationships are what push us to grow outside our comfort zones.

With a bigger energetic capacity to cope with what life throws at you, you can not only find more ease within yourself but also be strong enough to serve as a pillar, a shoulder to cry on. When a friend or partner or family member is going through their own tough time, even a dark night of the soul, you can be there to witness and hold, without feeling fear, pushing away, or trying to fix. You'll also be less likely to become embroiled in other people's drama, and you'll notice when your healthy boundaries are disintegrating and you are becoming the company that misery loves or, even more problematic, becoming a misery vampire, someone who feeds on others' despair. You'll be less likely to listen to the news and fall into a state of apathy. Instead, you'll do something.

There will be a time when you or someone close to you is facing a loss—of a loved one, an animal, a home, a job, an identity, a belief system, a life as you or they knew it. There will be times when you have to make a really hard decision, confront a tough diagnosis, or face a traumatic event. How will you use your tools to support yourself, your loved ones, your coven? You will source embodied strength and wisdom from your prior tipping-point life experiences, from your lived experiences. You will not shy away from the pain, the despair, the fear, because you've become intimate with your emotions; you've learned that the way to the other side is through. You've found your own strength and courage before, and you will guide your loved ones to find theirs. You have cultivated your own capacity to hold space and develop compassion for yourself and others. You won't just provide lip service or platitudes but will show up with your deeply felt presence and vulnerability. You will know when you need to take care of yourself first—by meditating, clearing your energy, practicing self-care, giving yourself space to cry or scream, or giving yourself a hug. You will communicate your boundaries, needs, and emotional capacity without guilt—your open-hearted, deep, embodied presence requires this. Every trial you experience or witness is an invitation to ask yourself: "Where do I have to grow or expand in my life?"

REFLECTION

- Have you ever experienced a dark night of the soul? Did you know it was a dark night of the soul at the time? Describe the experience.
- How did you resist your dark night of the soul? How did you surrender?
- What did you learn about yourself as a result of your dark night of the soul?
- Did you grieve the loss of parts of your identity?
- Did you gain any tools for the trial? Make a list and remind yourself of how far you've come.
- What is your capacity to support others and be of service while not losing yourself?

- What allows you to drop into a deeper meditative state? Is it movement before sitting? Is it music or chanting? Is it a guided meditation or pranayama (yogic breath control)?
- Do you allow your body and your intuition to guide you to what you need? Do you know your spirit guides? Have you received guidance that you know came from a higher source? How did these messages come through to you?

CHAPTER 4

YOUR SPIRITUAL PRACTICE DOESN'T NEED TO LOOK ONE WAY

There is a voice that doesn't use words. Listen!
—Rumi

Spirituality is the practice of learning and unlearning, of healing and growing, of accepting and surrendering. As we are each having our own unique human experience, our spiritual paths and therefore our healing are also unique.

We have each already gained wisdom from our many previous lives, and this innate wisdom of our true self is always available to us—we just have to awaken and remember. Just think about all that you have been through already: everything you have experienced, what you have overcome, the people that you have loved and lost—over multiple lifetimes. All of this has caused you to evolve and grow at the soul level. We still have so much to learn and heal from; that is our calling in this lifetime. We chose to come back to earth school to learn lessons to further advance our souls, but we as Women in Total Conscious Healing are also here during this exact time in our evolution to share the wisdom and light that is already shining so bright within us.

To do so, we must find tools, techniques, practices, and rituals for our daily lives. Our timelines, awakenings, energetic upgrades, and experiences are going to be so very different as we create our unique spiritual practices. That is why we cannot compare our own path with that of others or copy the way someone else lives their life and expect to evolve and learn the lessons we are meant to learn. If our spiritual practices are helping us with our healing transformation, then copying someone's spiritual practice is like copying someone else's healing journey and wondering why it isn't working. Well, because it isn't yours. The practices aren't aligned to your current experience and aren't intuitively integrated.

For example, say you are dealing with sexual trauma. The practice that might resonate with you could be a form of inner-child therapy or talk therapy, while a spiritual practice that entails sexual expansion such as tantra or orgasmic meditation might initially be unhelpful, even triggering. Maybe you will be called to those practices at a later point in your healing journey; maybe not. What works for someone else won't necessarily work for you, and vice versa. (I am in no way giving advice here on how to deal with sexual trauma; please seek help from a professional if you are struggling.)

You might say that this is obvious, but we are raised in and conditioned by a society that tries really hard to create a one-size-fits-all model for life. We move through the school system from kindergarten to high school, go to college or get a job, find a partner, get married, procreate, work to pay bills, and die. At least that is what a "normal" and "successful" life should look like, according to the status quo.

Is this really why we are here? I used to think so. I fully subscribed to this model of capitalistic success, of collecting degrees, certifications, titles, and medals. I set priorities around doing and achieving, and I doggedly pursued outward success. Until one day, I finally got to the point where I had to honestly ask myself this question: *Is this all there is to life?*

Of course not. I eventually woke up to the fact that there is so much more to life, and to my own being, than that which I was taught and made to believe. I woke up to the fact that I have free will and choice. Not everyone does in the way that my education and income and skin color afford me. Investing time and money to find oneself is most certainly a privilege.

Just as we are all unique and have our own journeys, being on a spiritual path is like walking a tightrope. To paraphrase Jesus, it is like being in this world but not of this world. While we must do what we need to survive in this world, our true selves and our consciousnesses are not of this world and therefore not bound by it. We can choose to not let conditioning and fearmongering run our lives.

Easier said than done.

WALKING A TIGHTROPE

At the time of this writing, I am in my mid to late thirties, unmarried, and without children. Given that, people make a lot of assumptions about my choices, about who I am. People assume that I chose my career and money over love and family, that I am a witch in the pejorative sense of the word: a selfish woman, a woman who doesn't conform to social norms, a woman hungry for money and power, an unnatural woman.

Eye roll.

Sadly, the pressure to abide by certain timelines and socially acceptable or "successful" choices causes many of us a great deal of pain and despair. I'd be the first to argue that it's perfectly acceptable to be an unmarried, child-free woman in her late thirties, or at any age. There are so many wonderful opportunities, there is so much freedom to explore, and we are lucky to not be forced into traditional social structures. That being said, I would really love to experience being a mother.

Although I fully trust in Divine timing and believe that I will be a mother someday (not just because I have had very vivid visions, but because I feel it), I also have to factor in my biological age. In this scenario, I'm pitting Divine timing against biological age, my trust in the Universe against the realities of the body. This is the tightrope.

For almost two years, I fell into a spiral of fearful thinking about running out of time and missing my opportunity. I went back and forth in my mind, asking myself, *Should I have a child on my own? Should I start accepting that it might not happen? Should I freeze my eggs?* With those ego-driven *should I's* came self-pity, shame, and more thoughts, like *How did I end up here? How did I let this happen? Do I not deserve to have a family? Is there something about me that is fundamentally unlovable?*

Practical issues: single motherhood, freezing eggs, not being a mother.

Spiritual issues: self-pity, FOMO, shame around life choices.

Then there was the issue of money. In my immigrant family, life revolved around working hard to survive. I grew up with the mindset that "money doesn't grow on trees," that "you have to work hard for what you want," and that "nothing is ever handed to you." And while I do believe in the value of hard work, and I am proud of what my parents accomplished, these beliefs around money and abundance are somewhat limiting. Yes, money does equal security in a very real sense, and I was afraid to tap into my "hard-earned" savings. *What if I spent a large sum of money on freezing my eggs and then I got laid off? What if something terrible happened and I didn't have the resources to deal with it? What if I spent all this money and never used the eggs?* With those thoughts came the catastrophizing, the fear-based, ego-driven thinking. *What if everything I've worked so hard for disappears? What if the bottom drops out and there's nothing and no one to catch me?*

Practical issue: spending savings on freezing eggs.

Spiritual issues: fear about safety and security, scarcity mindset.

Some might say that I should just have faith and trust. But the idea of freezing my eggs never left me, which was how I knew I had to do something. Nagging and persistent thoughts are often ways in which our spirit teams communicate to guide us. I had to decide to either act on the thought that just wouldn't leave me alone or sit back and wait. In other words, I had to decide to surrender in an active way or surrender in a more passive way, by not doing anything. Either way, a surrendering within my internal state was called for—whether I acted or not, I had no choice but to hand it over to the Universe.

But first, I had to face those nagging spiritual issues. Oh, my dear self-pity and shame. By the time I was contending with the dilemma of my biological clock versus Divine timing, many of the women in my coven were walking that same tightrope. When sharing and helping each other process, I realized that I really felt shame and pity only for myself, not for them. I was positive and encouraging, proud of their life choices—for leaving relationships that weren't serving them, for pursuing career opportunities they worked hard for and earned, for being dedicated to personal growth and development above all else, for forging their own paths on their own timelines. Having a community of women who could empathize with each other allowed me to realize that I am not the only one facing this; there is nothing wrong with me, and we are all on our own timeline. I am proud of the full life I have lived. It helped me release the shame I was feeling. I also took a step back and looked at my spiritual issues with money. I realized that I saw money as a finite or limited resource, something I struggled to obtain and that I was scared to let go of, even to let it do its job, thereby blocking the flow of abundance that is available to all of us. I recognized that holding on to or hoarding money out of fear sent a signal to the Universe that I didn't trust I would be taken care of. That no matter how much money was in my savings account, I couldn't buy time, security, love, or freedom. And that money is simply energy and therefore infinite.

My spiritual mentor, Janet, with her vast library, had just the right book for me. She handed me Tosha Silver's *It's Not Your Money: How to Live Fully from Divine Abundance.* In the book, Tosha talks about using one's abundance to demonstrate faith. This helped me reframe the idea of spending a large sum of money; I went from feeling loss and insecurity to having faith that what needed to come from this would: that I would learn the lesson I needed to learn, that more abundance would flow my way, that the money needed to change hands for one reason or another. I also reframed my thinking to be grateful for having savings in the first place. I stopped seeing my choice as a burden; rather, it was a blessing. I made a deal with myself to not obsess over the numbers on the medical bills or prescription costs, to simply look at them so I would know what to pay, and to remain in a state of gratitude. Each time I had to pay a bill, I would say a silent prayer to myself: *I am grateful to have the money to pay this bill, and I trust that this is exactly what I am supposed to be doing with it.*

This is walking the tightrope of being in the world but not of the world. I took that stubborn nagging thought as a sign that I was being guided by Spirit to take action. Once I had worked through my limiting beliefs around money and released the shame I felt, I used my spiritual tools to get clarity from that voice within, from my intuition. I meditated on it, I journaled about it, I confided in my coven, and I used my pendulum, my oracle cards, and my psychic skills to listen to any downloads or intuitive pings. The way it works for me is that even if my pendulum swings a clear "yes," I won't trust it unless it also comes with a strong "yes" from within, my inner guidance system. For me, the right decision was to go ahead and freeze my eggs.

Ultimately, there is never a "wrong" decision; we might just end up taking a more scenic route. I knew this was the right decision for me because as soon as I went through with it, the nagging thoughts and fears left me, and I felt relieved, even though my biological age and my financial and personal circumstances hadn't changed.

All of us have signed up to live during this time and to experience life within this matrix for a variety of reasons. Disappointment, frustration, grief, shame, and confusion all serve to awaken us. We are awakening to the facts that we get to choose, we get to create the life we want, and one path isn't better than another. One choice isn't better than another. One type of love isn't better than another—it is simply love. One spiritual practice isn't better than any other. What is important is that it is the right one for *you*.

Walking the tightrope is using your inner guidance system to navigate the physical and nonphysical realms. You might be contemplating leaving a life behind—a home, a relationship, financial security—to pursue an unknown path because your inner nagging is so strong. You are walking a tightrope of leaving everything you've built behind for something you cannot yet hold, see, or quantify. You might choose to fight a health issue with a combination of Western and Eastern medicine as well as holistic healing practices, acknowledging the benefits as well as limitations of science.

For me, the decision to freeze my eggs was about having a clear vision and sending a clear message to the Universe that I am choosing to be a mother. I had to align my energetic vibrations (mindset, beliefs, etc.), my resources (money, community), and my actions in this physical world with the spiritual guidance I received.

This was the spiritual practice, which was completely unique to me and specific to my situation. No one else would have addressed the decision in the same way, working with the same set of circumstances and conditioning. I built my spiritual practice to heal and gain more clarity—while putting the guidance I received into action. This is walking the tightrope of living in a participatory Universe.

SPIRITUAL BOOT CAMP

You might be asking yourself right now what a spiritual practice is, if what you are already doing qualifies as one, or where to even start.

A spiritual practice is taking regular action to cultivate spiritual development or induce spiritual experiences. Chances are that you already have a few in your repertoire. Most of us grew up performing spiritual practices at home or in a church, synagogue, temple, or mosque. You've likely said at least one or two prayers in your life: "Thank God" or "Holy shit!"

You might be subconsciously performing spiritual practices without knowing it, like making your morning coffee a ritual that includes some personal quiet time and reflection. Or maybe you like to take your shoes off and feel the soft grass under your feet. Oh yes, those count as spiritual practices.

On the path of becoming Women in Total Conscious Healing, there comes a point when we want to know more about the meaning of it all. We just might pick up that book that caught our eye at the neighborhood bookstore or sign up for that lecture at the meditation center down the street, without really knowing what it is that we are looking for.

Once we awaken and set foot on our spiritual path, and our reality as we know it starts to crumble, we usually enter into a stage that I like to call spiritual boot camp. Some might have a traumatizing experience that causes them to awaken, others find their way there by listening to their inner nagging or intuition, and still others awaken to their energetic gifts seemingly overnight. No matter how you end up peeking behind the veil, chances are that you won't ever be able to see the world as you did before.

Slowly but surely, we follow the white rabbit. We dabble, get overly excited, consume everything we can. We go on a quest to understand more and to become immersed in all things spiritual. There is a longing to spend more time on the other side of the veil because at your core it just feels so right. For me this started during my Saturn return. Isolated and depressed, I initially tried to run away from my feelings, trying to fix them by staying busy, overworking, and looking for solutions outside of myself. Eventually, my intuition got loud enough that I realized I needed to look within.

But where to start? I wanted to read every book, attend every course or retreat, and follow every teacher. Over the course of the following two or three years, I dove into my spiritual boot camp. I attended lectures at the Spiritualist Church of New York City, taking classes on intuitive awareness, psychic development, and Reiki. I got book recommendations and read about the soul's journey and purpose, the laws of the Universe, energetic and psychic powers, and how to manifest. I went on retreats. I took meditation, yoga, and breathwork classes. I sat in the audience when the likes of Marianne Williamson and Gabby Bernstein took to the stage in NYC. I soaked up everything I could and was hungry for more.

It was invigorating and eye-opening, but the more I learned, the more I also felt cheated. How had I not known all this before? Why weren't more people talking about it? Why weren't we taught any of this in school? And then my ego started piping in. *Why does everyone else seem to know so much more than me? How am I ever going to catch up? How do I know which is the right teaching or tool?* What is *the* solution to my problems, *the* perfect answer to my questions? And with that, I had officially entered the phase of spiritual overwhelm.

SPIRITUAL OVERWHELM

Still very much hostage to my conditioning, my inner people-pleasing perfectionist wanted to study hard and get all As. I wanted to practice, like the athlete I am, to improve my psychic gifts. There were no trophies or medals to be won, but I was still determined to win them.

Don't get me wrong. Developing a spiritual practice does require dedication, consistency, and a willingness to learn. Focusing on the outcome, however, is futile.

For me, realizing that the "test" is actually a lifelong series of experiences and lessons, and that we practice and learn without always having a concrete goal, was overwhelming. How was I supposed to know when I'd made it if there was no grade or degree or medal to tell me?

The sense of overwhelm increased when I tried to follow every spiritual teacher and influencer who crossed my path, at times even putting certain teachers on a pedestal. They were so radiant, so perfect, so much more evolved than the rest of us. Far, far more evolved than I was. There were so many coaches and gurus out there promising certain outcomes, and I was sure that all I had to do was follow as many teachings as possible to a T. Then doubt and decision paralysis crept in. What if, in this maze of spiritual paths, I didn't follow the "right" one?

This is, of course, a trap, which I have fallen into more than once. I signed up for a program because I felt like I should, because I felt inadequate and insecure, or because I was trying to control an outcome or timing. I clicked the bait before taking a moment to get back into alignment or recognize my fear-based thinking. In those instances, when I chose from fear or desperation, I usually didn't get what I was hoping for, or I wasn't actually ready to do the internal work that was required of me. Because, let's face it, there is no golden ticket or magic program—you still need to do the work.

How many times have you bought a program because you thought you should or that you desperately needed it? How many of those courses did you buy because the marketing spoke directly to your fears and desperation? How many of those programs or courses did you actually finish?

There have been times, though, when I have been lucky and (I believe) guided to a program, lecture, or teacher that exposed me to something I didn't even know I needed. Those have always been the most beneficial experiences for me, because the teachings or tools usually aligned with exactly where I was in my spiritual development.

Again, don't get me wrong: I am a huge believer in the value of learning ancient practices and traditions as well as learning from the experience of others. I think it is powerful to work with coaches who can help us notice our blind spots or hold space for our healing. It is even more powerful to sit in a circle with plugged-in individuals, share a sacred space, and be witnessed in our evolution. The only way to know if a practice or teacher or community is right for you is to try it. Don't think of it as a waste of time—there is no scarcity of time, and every new experience is worthwhile. The scenic route may take longer, but think of the view! Anyway, there is no rush and no arrival, so why take the expressway?

Everything we are taught has been taught before. Ancient

wisdom resonates with its audience when it is packaged in the life experience and vibration of the channel, or teacher, who is relaying it. Some of you will identify with my experiences and find value in this book, for example, and some of you might think what I am sharing is a whole load of crap. That is OK and actually expected.

No teaching, method, or ceremony is more valuable than our own internal knowing. No teacher, guru, coach, parent, shaman, or pastor knows you better than you know yourself. Any healer and teacher worth their salt will teach you exactly how powerful you already are and how to access that power for yourself.

When we feel ourselves becoming overwhelmed, the single most important thing to do is to listen within. What is your body telling you? What is your guidance telling you? What is important on our spiritual path is to get to a point where we can sift through the vast amount of information that is available to us and choose that which *feels* right in our heart and gut, right for where we are in our life curriculum. Teachers, books, and courses will (often synchronously) find us when the time is right. We don't have to force it. One size does not fit all. A resounding *yes* feels expansive, exciting, and just right.

SPIRITUAL BYPASSING

In the early 1980s, Buddhist teacher and psychotherapist John Welwood introduced the term "spiritual bypassing" and defined it as a "tendency to use spiritual ideas and practices to sidestep or avoid facing unresolved emotional issues, psychological wounds, and unfinished developmental tasks." Using spiritual practice as a defense mechanism or a tool for avoidance might make us feel better in the short term, and sometimes we truly do need to pause and collect ourselves before facing conflict or wounding. Sometimes we need to manage the symptoms of post-traumatic stress before we can deal with the causes. But if all we do is de-escalate and self-soothe, then we cannot grow. If we only gloss over issues, reduce immediate stress, pacify our egos, or avoid triggers, then we will stay stuck.

Mindfulness principles that simply focus on accessing presence through awareness and stillness can be a way to perpetuate avoidance and detachment. Presence is great as long as it is not used to avoid the shadow elements of the human experience, make one feel superior, or avoid taking action because "it is what it is."

Recognizing spiritual bypassing can be difficult because it can be quite subtle. Chances are that you have done it. I know I have. It can be meditating instead of communicating, praying instead of taking direct action. It can take the form of telling someone that "everything happens for a reason" or that they are being overly negative when they are expressing pain. Often this kind of reaction is a helpful red flag that reveals the dismissive person's discomfort with difficult emotions. Toxic positivity, the belief that we should put a positive spin even on tragic events, and incessant optimism don't leave room for working through negative emotions, and ignoring negative emotions can lead to worse problems in the long term. This looks like asserting, "It could be worse," instead of validating emotional experience, or telling someone that failure is not an option. Instead of "It could be worse," try saying, "That really sucks. I am sorry you're going through this. Is there anything I can do for you?"

Emotions are neither positive nor negative; they just are. Being spiritual means honoring our shadow self and answering the call of pain, anger, sadness, rage, shame, guilt, and grief when it shows itself like a serpent emerging from its hiding place. This is the good, deep, and messy part of us— the raw and real. We didn't incarnate to earth to be perfect or palatable. We came to experience life, to grow, to fail and make mistakes, to let go, to heal trauma, and to have our hearts cracked wide open. We came to feel deeply and to forge authentic relationships.

For example, anger is a perfectly fine emotion in certain situations. It is totally acceptable to be angry at the person who hurt you, to be furious at the way our reproductive rights are being curtailed, to be mad when your male colleague is getting paid more than you, to be upset when your partner doesn't follow through on an important obligation. Spiritual bypassing can stifle relationships if we avoid dealing with difficult emotions and the behaviors that caused the problematic situation in the first place. Authentic spirituality fosters authentic expression of all emotions, even if they are uncomfortable.

In order to grow as human and spiritual beings and to be fully present, we need to welcome all parts of ourselves. Real presence isn't mind-centric but heart-centric, and heart-centric healing requires us to witness our emotions and then transform them through expression and release. Regardless of who or what might have sparked our anger or grief, it is our personal responsibility to find practices that allow us to grow through deep, embodied feelings and to learn healthy ways to respond.

Just like our sexual selves don't have much place to roam in this world, neither do our shadow selves.

—*Alexandra Roxo*

TRY THIS: MAKE YOUR SHADOW YOUR FRIEND

STEP 1: DO THE WORK AND AVOID SPIRITUAL BYPASSING.

Your spiritual practices should support your transformation, not replace the hard work of getting to the depth of your wounds. Get curious and examine your current practices.

- Do you only ever meditate or pray when you need to soothe yourself?
- Do you repress or override negative thoughts and feelings?
- What toxically positive statements do you use? How can you reframe them?

STEP 2: FIND AN OUTLET TO EXPRESS YOUR EMOTIONS.

Give your emotions space to express in a healthy way.

- Name the emotion you are feeling. Sit with the emotion without judgment and simply observe. What does it feel like? Is there a color or memory associated with this feeling? Where in your body do you experience this feeling and how?
- Ask yourself what you need, and give yourself the space to express. This can be ugly-crying, taking a boxing class, screaming into a pillow until you surrender in a beautiful puddle of your own tears, taking a cold shower, or calling a friend.

STEP 3: FIND A FRIEND OR COMMUNITY
THAT CAN HOLD SPACE.

- Do you have someone in your life who has a healthy expression of emotions? Someone who is good at communicating what they feel? This person could also be your therapist, coach, or role model.
- Once you have identified a person you feel safe with, practice sharing what you are feeling. If you've never talked about your true feelings, then this might be hard at first, but don't give up. It is liberating for all parts of us to be seen.

STEP 4: SET BOUNDARIES.

Honor your emotions and listen to your body. Pay attention to how people, situations, and surroundings make you feel and then learn to honor those emotions by setting boundaries. It is OK to say no, and sometimes the most spiritual thing you can do is to politely tell someone to "Fuck off!"

SPIRITUAL RESISTANCE

Sometimes we get tired of doing the work.

Of course, the spiritual path is joyous, beautiful, expansive, and enlightening, but to truly go deep requires courage and persistence. There is always another layer to uncover, and at times we get pushed to the edge of our endurance.

The first time I encountered this was about three years into my spiritual journey. Within a nine-month time span, I had traveled to Germany to take care of my mother during her cancer treatment and gone through a breakup. I was emotionally drained and needed time away to disconnect and find myself again. So I decided on a whim to join friends on a trip to Bali. I also booked a three-day silent retreat before I'd be joining the other girls for some adventure.

The silent retreat was in the middle of nowhere surrounded by rice paddies. My accommodation was a concrete hut, a simple bed with a mosquito net, and a shower with a toilet in it. I had no access to my phone or the internet, no caffeine or sugar, and nobody to talk to. We could participate in daily meditation and yoga at 6:00 a.m. and 2:00 p.m.; otherwise, we were left alone with our thoughts.

I'd brought a coloring book and Michael Newton's *Journey of Souls*, which I'd read a few years prior. I slept and read for a good portion of the first twenty-four hours. The more I read about the journey of souls and grasped the concept that we are never done learning and evolving at the soul level, the more defeated I felt. I was already so tired that the thought of continuous lessons and healing work just felt insurmountable. It was a full-body tiredness, like I had cement in my veins instead of blood. I laid the book down, rolled over onto my back, and decided to just be alone with my thoughts. Once I stopped and simply surrendered, I started to purge, a whole-body release of emotions but also physically purging. Everything that I had pushed down in order to emotionally function that year came back up. I spent two full days alone in that concrete hut, unable to eat or participate in the meditation or yoga sessions.

What I thought would be a relaxing, spiritual time to rest and reset was quite the opposite. My body was saying in no uncertain terms, "Nope. We've reached maximum capacity. We're done. There will be no more learning today."

Nobody can do deep work all the time. Sometimes the best thing you can do is stop what you're doing and wait it out. Give yourself time to integrate. You can always pick back up where you left off when the time is right.

INTEGRATION

There is no graduation from spiritual boot camp, and it's likely you'll experience spiritual overwhelm or FOMO and spiritual exhaustion more than once. With consistent practice, however, we develop and strengthen our intuitive muscles, and we learn to trust that we know what it is that we need. Discernment can only truly come with experience. From the more general broad-stroke teachings, we move into spiritual practices that are more aligned with our current earthly assignment.

We will continue to be guided to experiences, teachers, books, and relationships that get into those deeper, unknown layers of ourselves. For me, at one time this took the form of dancing to EDM to the point of falling into a trancelike state. At other times, I craved quiet meditation with a silent mantra or deep visualization exercises. Sometimes I journal and practice automatic writing every day; sometimes I don't. Sometimes I work with my tools of divination, such as crystals, pendulums, and oracle cards; sometimes I don't.

We will continue to uncover more of our hidden parts, our deep-seated wounds, secrets, desires, and gifts. We continually embark on a deeper level of healing and expansion, if we choose to heed the call to become Women in Total Conscious Healing.

In this phase, we also start to remember, to awaken the cellular memory that already holds the wisdom of the higher self that we've accumulated throughout our lifetimes. This might manifest itself in an affinity for certain ancient practices and ceremonies that feel comfortable or natural to you, as if you have done them before. Chances are you have. You might recognize certain cultures or places as sacred and holy, as if you have been there before. The longer you are on your spiritual path, the more will be uncovered and revealed to you. Stay curious and willing to adapt—your spiritual evolution depends on it.

My cellular soul memory was activated in Pompeii in 2019. I was on a lovely two-week vacation on the Amalfi Coast, and my friend and I decided to spend one day visiting Pompeii, an ancient city decimated by the eruption of Mount Vesuvius in 79 CE. I hadn't been there before, but I did study Latin for eight years in high school and, with my class, translated ancient texts that occasionally mentioned Pompeii.

My friend and I joined a guided tour, and one of the stops was at an intersection. The guide explained how the streets were constructed, and although this was interesting, it wasn't extremely exciting. And what I was feeling was excitement— an intense feeling running through my entire body. So intense, in fact, that it caught me off guard. I paused for a moment, closing my eyes and tuning in. What was this feeling?

I was feeling excited to be back. My soul recognized this street, this location. I had been there before.

This was a very intense experience of synchronicity, of a sense of connection between two seemingly disconnected events, and déjà vu, a feeling of familiarity in seemingly new or unusual experiences. Both have an enormous amount of spiritual wisdom and guidance to offer, if we are open to it.

We continued to the next stop, the ruin of the Doric temple that used to be the sanctuary to the Greek goddess Athena. As the guide explained the history and how the temple was destroyed with the destruction of the goddess culture, I became angry. Angry like it was a personal attack. Again, I was caught off guard by the intensity of this feeling.

Back at the hotel that evening, those moments of remembrance still in my bones, I confided in my friend about what had transpired. Thankfully, she didn't think this was completely insane. We had a good chat with some rosé, overlooking the beautiful scene of the Amalfi Coast from the balcony of the hotel bar. The Mediterranean Sea reflected the twinkling lights of Sorrento and Naples as we talked.

That same year, I was studying to become an ordained minister in the Spiritualist Church. One of my teachers and now dear friend, Janet, came up to me at the beginning of one of our earlier classes and handed me a book. "I was told by my guides that you needed to read this book," she said. I looked at the cover. *When God Was a Woman*—oh, what a title!

I had never asked Janet why she thought I needed to read it. But after that experience in Pompeii, I understood that there was a connection. In our next class, I told her about my feelings and what they meant to me—that I had lived there in a previous life. She looked at me, a confused expression on her face. "Yes, of course," she said. "You lived as a high priestess during those times, and you were worshipped for your contributions to the goddess religion. I thought you knew that already."

I didn't. I had to walk the streets I used to walk and visit the temple where I used to practice to have that awakening.

Integration occurs naturally when you are ready. There are periods of seeking new knowledge, reading books, and taking courses, and periods of being with what you've discovered. I was guided to Merlin Stone's *When God Was a Woman*, then had an experience that showed me the connection and its significance, the Divine feminine on the page and the Divine feminine in life. What a revelation.

The phases of developing our spiritual practice are part of a nonlinear, cyclical process of awakening, overwhelm, integration, stagnation, resistance, and reawakening—it is continuous and ever-evolving. During each of those phases your spiritual practice will look different. And the more you allow yourself to "follow the white rabbit" into new depths of yourself and the collective consciousness, the more personal and integrated your practices will become. There is no perfection in spiritual practice. The most important aspect of any spiritual practice is that it is in alignment with your own healing and feels integrated and embodied, allowing you to find balance between staying consistent and staying curious so that your practice evolves naturally. Getting to this level of trust and knowing within yourself takes time and practice.

We call it spiritual *practice* for a reason.

As a Woman in Total Conscious Healing, you will learn to trust your intuition, your body, and your spirit team to guide you. You will find which environments, teachers, practices, songs, or types of touch help you access the Divine. It can even be as simple as asking yourself: "What makes me feel good/alive/joyous, or turned on?"

My hope is that you feel empowered to explore and figure out what resonates with you and how certain practices make you feel. Because feeling all the feelings authentically is what creates connection to the Divine. Your spiritual practice is personal and ever-evolving. It can be all things because *you are all things.*

DÉJÀ VU

Déjà vu gives us a glimpse into our eternal wisdom, our consciousness. A glimpse into what is always there but not always accessible to us in our human form.

While there are many scientific theories about déjà vu, I believe that it is both a memory and a psychic phenomenon, that our soul, together with our guides, plans out the life that we are meant to live during this incarnation. One psychic theory is that during the planning process, we leave ourselves bread crumbs along the path, like mile markers, reminding us that we are right where we are supposed to be, with whomever we are supposed to be, doing exactly what we should be doing—because we planned it that way. Déjà vu is therefore a spiritual cue that everything is unfolding according to plan.

I personally believe that there is some guidance or insight to be gleaned from having such a "glitch in the matrix" type of experience. And, as someone who will forever be a skeptic, I believe that everyone gets to choose the belief or theory that most fits their own spiritual practice. It is no different with déjà vu. You even get to choose not to assign any greater meaning to it at all and to simply take the experience for what it is worth.

The following are different beliefs about déjà vu. As with any intuitive hit, pay close attention and take the time to reflect to glean meaning and potential guidance.

- Recalling memories from a past life: Déjà vu experiences might be encounters from a past life, reminding you of you who were and that there is wisdom and experience you can access beyond what you are aware of in this lifetime. This wisdom can help you with a particular issue you are facing in your current life.

- Messages from your higher self: Déjà vu experiences are reminders of your path and mission on earth, often called "golden nuggets" or bread crumbs that you have left yourself to help with your awareness of your purpose. Use them to overcome challenges.

- Precognitive dreams: The sense of familiarity in a déjà vu experience might be because you dreamed of this situation before. Precognitive dreams show you events that are bound to happen at some point in the future.

- Parallel lives: You might have watched this event unfold on a different timeline, meaning that the familiarity felt with déjà vu is due to timeline shifts.

• Guidance from guides, angels, and ancestors: Déjà vu experiences are messages guiding you and supporting you through challenging moments in the present.

TRY THIS: FINDING MEANING THROUGH DÉJÀ VU

If you believe that there is some guidance or insight to be gleaned from having a déjà vu experience, then you might ask yourself some questions to help you get clear on what it means to you.

First, recall any past "glitch in the matrix" type of experience that you have had in your lifetime. Then write down your answers to the following questions:

• What triggered this experience?
• How did it make me feel?
• What was the memory about (if it triggered a specific memory)?
• How can this experience influence my life in a positive way?

REFLECTION

• Did you go through a spiritual boot camp? Describe that experience.
• Have you experienced spiritual overwhelm? How about spiritual resistance?
• How many courses have you subscribed to that you never finished or that didn't actually resonate with you? What need were you trying to fill?

- Have you put certain teachers on a pedestal? If so, what insecurity or doubt were you trying to alleviate?
- Have you used spiritual practices and courses as a crutch because you don't yet trust your own inner knowing? Have you used spiritual practices to distract you from doing the deep inner work?
- Have you ever used spiritual bypassing? When? What were your motives?
- Have you ever reached a point of spiritual exhaustion? What did that look like for you?
- Are you conscious and discerning about what practices you decide to integrate and why? What are you trying to achieve? Is it healing, calming the mind, or connecting with a source greater than you?
- What are the moments when you feel most in your body? What brings you the most joy? What brings you the most peace?
- When do you feel most connected to the Divine?

CHAPTER 5

CREATING YOUR COVEN

Growing up, I felt very much that I belonged. I felt at home when with family, at school, in church, and in the fencing community (before I was asked to switch allegiance to countries). I lived comfortably in different cultures from a young age—my father was Irish, my mother was Scottish, and we lived in Germany—and my personal identity was never tied solely to a particular group. My father was the one who took us to church; my mother was agnostic and didn't join us, and my grandmother was a psychic medium, someone who is able to raise their own energetic vibrations (e.g., through meditation and clearing energies from their aura), to recognize or tune in to the vibrations from Spirit and convey messages and guidance. In fact, I come from a long lineage of psychic mediums. My great-aunt was a well-known medium in Scotland, my uncle was gifted in psychometry (the ability to read the energy of an object), my cousin hears Spirit, and my sister sees Spirit, just to name a few.

In my household, it was a given that our spirituality was a personal journey. My grandmother was the first person I knew who was a psychic medium, and it was something completely normal for us—but I didn't understand yet that it also related to a belief system. At the time, all I knew was that I didn't agree with the outdated doctrine of Catholicism. I hadn't yet discovered my psychic abilities or the principles of spiritualism, and I honestly didn't recognize the importance of a particular belief system for me personally. So I spent years without any formal religious participation; or, rather, fencing and academic achievement were my religion. Within these realms, I thrived.

Things changed once I was ostracized by the German team for my Irish citizenship. Still, I maintained some of those relationships, and I made friends as a student athlete in the US. When I got to the Olympic Games, however, I realized that I didn't know a single person on the Irish Olympic team, the team for which I was competing. When patriotism was on full display, I never felt more out of place.

A few years later, when I was finishing graduate school, I applied to twelve job opportunities across the United States, in Boston, Chicago, San Francisco, Los Angeles, and New York City. I had interviews at almost all these places, and ended up getting three offers, all in NYC. Coincidence? I don't think so. Now the only decision left to make was which job to take, since my next location had already been decided.

They say that New York City attracts people in search of something, that it's a place that will take you to your edge. I clearly needed to be in this dense, energetic space for the next phase of my awakening.

For the next two years, I mainly focused on launching my career. My job as a management consultant kept me away from NYC every Monday through Thursday, and that lifestyle didn't lend itself to building a community, especially in a new place. I didn't have much of a social life, besides a few friends I knew from college who had already established their own circles.

I remember starting to feel isolated and lonely, burned out

and depressed. I got lost in the rat race, the glitz and glam, the endless agitation of the city. On the weekends, I would spend time with people I didn't really like just to not feel so alone. But that actually made me lonelier.

One day, out of the blue, I decided to get a psychic reading. I had never gotten a reading before, even though my grandmother was a medium. It can be difficult to read objectively for a family member or someone well known to us, our own emotions and knowledge clouding the information we receive psychically or from Spirit. She understood this.

I was desperate for guidance, and my stack of new self-help books wasn't doing it for me. On top of that, I had a really strong longing to connect with my grandmother, who had passed away more than a decade earlier. So I googled "psychic mediums in NYC," read a few profiles, and was drawn to one lady in particular. A week later, we met via Skype. I had prepared questions as instructed: "Why am I feeling so stuck? What should my next step be in life? Will I meet someone special? What does my grandmother have to share with me?" Basically, the standard questions for a first reading. After an opening prayer and a short meditation, before we even got to any of my questions, she had already connected with my grandmother. I was hanging on to every word as she conveyed my grandmother's voice, so familiar and comforting. It felt good to know she was still around and aware of the happenings in my life. I received the guidance and reassurance I was looking for, and the psychic helped me understand what it was that I was going through. I wasn't depressed; I was awakening and right where I needed to be.

She asked me, "Do you know that you are psychic?" Before I could answer, I had a clear feeling in my solar plexus, my gut.

"Hmm, no, not really?" I replied, but my body was saying, *Oh* yes!

"Your grandmother wants you to know that you don't need

to go through anyone else," she went on, "and that you already know how to contact her."

I did? How? I was confused and intrigued.

Toward the end of the reading, I mentioned that I was searching for a community and that I wanted to learn more about my energetic gifts and this ability to connect with my late grandmother. The psychic recommended that I pay a visit to the Spiritualist Church of New York City. As a lapsed Catholic, I found the word *church* an immediate turnoff. Weeks went by, and I did nothing with the psychic's suggestion. After a few more weeks of feeling lost and with nothing to lose, I decided to attend one of their Sunday-evening lectures—with as much of an open mind as possible.

The services were being held at Saint Albans Church in Murray Hill, on the east side of Manhattan. I felt extremely awkward as I opened the doors and walked inside. An usher handed me a book with songs and prayers. I sat down in a pew toward the back so I could observe, which is what I do best. Since the Spiritualist Church only rented the space for their services and lectures, they put a beautiful big picture of a sunflower in front of the altar. I later learned that the sunflower is a symbol for spiritualism and that their motto is: "As the sunflower turns its face to the light of the sun, so Spiritualism turns the face of humanity toward the light of truth."

After the invocation, they asked everyone to spend five minutes getting to know one another. *Oh, how awkward,* I thought. No longer being able to hide and observe, I shook hands, was welcomed by regulars, and exchanged a few "Oh, it's your first time here too? What brought you here?"

A female minister, dressed in business casual attire, got up to give a lecture. This was a far cry from my experiences in Catholic church. She explored the topic of trusting the Universe or Spirit and the real-life struggles that come with that. She even asked the congregation to weigh in and share their own insights and perspectives. It wasn't at all the type of church service I was used to. It wasn't preachy and didn't impose an outdated dogma or creed. Rather, it was educational and informational, and it allowed room for questions. I really liked it.

Here was a community of very diverse people from all different faiths, people like me who were simply curious or wanted to make sense of their burgeoning energetic gifts. I was fascinated. A religion based on conviction and not conversion? A religion that does not require anyone to change their view of God? A religion that is about inclusion and not separation? A religion that believes in the autonomous and authentic self? I learned that spiritualism isn't just a religion but also a science, a philosophy, and a way of life.

I started to understand what people meant when they said that they were spiritual. This community was like a breath of fresh air. Needless to say, I was intrigued.

After exploring different meditation and yoga practices and attending the Sunday lectures regularly, I wanted to learn more.

Mediumship and spiritualism have been an integral part of religious experience from primitive times to the present, I soon learned. The belief that the soul is separate from the physical body (animism) or that the communication from the spirit world or God is sacred could fall within the realm of spiritualism. Even the Bible mentions mediumship, as in the story of the Witch of Endor. There are many forerunners of modern American spiritualism. Emanuel Swedenborg (1688–1772) is credited with first positing that death of the physical body does not result in an immediate change in personality, since the spirit world is governed by natural law. German physician Franz Anton Mesmer (1734–1815) applied scientific principles to the human aura and mesmerism, hypnotism, therapeutic touch, and trance. The advent of modern spiritualism, however, arrived in 1848, when the Fox sisters established communication with Spirit and launched a major religious movement, which they later denounced.

Today, the National Spiritualist Association of Churches still uses the definition established in 1919, which describes spiritualism as a science, philosophy, and religion of continuous life. This continuity of life is made evident through mediumship and connection to the spirit world. (To learn more, head to https://nsac.org/what-we-believe/definining-spiritualism/.)

As I was doing this research, I kept thinking about my grandmother. She'd lived her life within the sphere of this science, philosophy, and religion, and now I was following in her footsteps. Around that same time, I received an email from the psychic announcing that she was rolling out a course about intuitive awareness and how to trust your own intuition. Well, there it was, another bread crumb leading me down the path of getting to know myself better. I signed up immediately.

I was hooked. I learned about the Spiritualist Church's sister organization, the Holistic Studies Institute, which offered psychic-development classes. I committed to ten full weekends over the course of a year to become certified as a psychic medium. I have never looked back.

The people I met during these courses viewed the world the same way that I do and were passionate about the same things: self-awareness, healing, spiritual growth, energetic gifts, service to the greater good. It was there that I met my spiritual mentors and found the community I was looking for. These people were my people, my *coven*.

FROM TRIBALISM TO CHOSEN COMMUNITY

Almost anything is possible when you have a safe place to bloom.
—Unknown

As humans and energetic beings, we are hardwired to need connection with others. Living with others, learning from one another, and creating community allows us to explore our own conscious identity. But before we are able to choose a group or community, our *coven*, we identify with the tribe—our family, culture, and religion—to which we are born.

As children, we are completely dependent on our tribe for survival. Our early social environment and our sense of belonging provide us with the structure to develop our emotional well-being. We naturally take on beliefs that keep that structure alive. An obvious example is an international sporting event like the Olympics. Athletes are meant to identify with their teammates; spectators identify with athletes from their country's team simply because they share a nationality.

Some believe that we choose our biological family and our circumstances from which to start our lives and, with that, our spiritual journeys. Our early circumstances and opportunities are therefore divinely chosen for us, so that we have the opportunity to learn how to overcome tribal thinking and conditioning and gain the courage to awaken to a more conscious and inclusive perspective. Eventually, some of us realize that many beliefs based on broad shared parameters actually create a narrow outlook, a tribalism designed to keep the structure of the family, community, parish, or culture separate from others.

As Ram Dass is credited with saying, "If you think you're enlightened, go spend a week with your family!" Even though I am very close with my family, I've still had to learn to identify our shared biases and worldview and let go of those that aren't authentically mine. I feel guilty setting boundaries, and I fear losing connection, but I have come to accept that my path is my own and that I do not need approval from my family or anyone for living my purpose, as only I, and my spirit team, know what this path is. Each member of my family has their own path, too, and we don't need to fully understand each other to accept, support, and love each other. This can be hard, as we all want to be fully known, seen, and understood by those closest to us, but we also have to remember that we don't all have the same perspective on the world we live in. And that's OK. As a people-pleasing perfectionist, I find this to be one of my greatest lessons, one which I continually learn and relearn. My family and I have a literal ocean between us, which allows me to continue to explore on my own. With them, and within my small hometown, I only have to test myself and my vulnerability to the tribalism and conditioning of my childhood every so often, when I go home for a visit.

The contradictions and friction inherent in experience and exposure to the unknown challenge us to see things differently and to step outside our comfort zones, to take an honest look at our beliefs, to discard the ones that no longer fit and hold on to those that do. We awaken to the fact that we are all part of one spiritual community, the Universe, and that we are all on a healing journey back to our inner truth. We let go of the trappings of identity. Those markers just don't matter all that much anymore.

As we follow our passions, we will organically meet the people with whom we align, spiritually and philosophically. We'll organically meet the people whom we simply like, for no particular reason or because some indescribable something just works. And we'll organically meet people who will test us.

EVERY RELATIONSHIP HAS A PURPOSE

When setting out on a journey, do not seek advice from those who have never left home.
—Rumi

Tipping-point life experiences give us an opportunity to choose to stagnate or to change. We can trade the pursuit of personal truth for a sense of belonging, resigning ourselves to the status quo in exchange for the potential of existential uncertainty. Or we choose to change, to muster the courage and willpower to let go of familiar beliefs and to choose groups and people that foster our growth as well as that of the collective.

This requires awareness of personal responsibility and how a truth not prescribed by social structures can serve the greater good. More importantly, this path requires that we find a way to anchor ourselves in self-trust and integrity, especially when life as we know it starts to seem fragile.

Of course, in the beginning, we can't always tell what is personal truth and what is tribalism or conditioning with a new hairdo. That's why it's a practice, and why making mistakes and turning down cul-de-sacs are just part of the process.

For a large chunk of my life, I searched for my truth in all the wrong places. Due to the lack of a relationship with myself, distrust in my own power, and ignorance of the Divine order of the Universe, I was susceptible to developing loyalty to people who didn't deserve it, all in an effort to belong.

With my sun sign in Leo, I am extremely loyal, a trait I take pride in. But it can turn toxic, especially when combined with my tendency to people-please. Many times I aligned myself with people or organizations who either didn't respect me or took advantage of me. I stayed loyal to coaches who didn't always have my best interests at heart. For eight years I stayed loyal to my first corporate job, only to find out that I was being paid $20,000 to $30,000 less than my peers, many of whom hadn't been at the company as long. I stayed loyal to a boss who offered me a position to work with her directly, only to be left stranded in an unfortunate political position. I stayed in romantic relationships longer than I should have.

Each of these situations had a lesson to teach me. We develop individual consciousness not in isolation; in every stage, we attract people and circumstances to help us uncover deeper layers of our own complexities. Relationships, no matter how long they last, all have their purpose. Even that six-hour relationship with the person sitting next to you on the plane or that two-minute relationship with the checkout guy at the grocery store can mean something. Relationships teach us about how we meet our own needs and how we resolve conflict with the self and others. Some relationships will conveniently end as you change or when you come out of the spiritual closet. Others will emerge when you start to show yourself more authentically. Some relationships will remain casual; others will go to a much deeper emotional level.

Some relationships will be painful. These relationships are often, though not always, present in our lives for divine reasons. Some people, often within our family of origin, trigger us in certain ways. Others come into our lives, cause emotional havoc, and leave just as quickly.

The karmic soul mate who sparked a dark night of the soul was one such person. How did I know that this person was a karmic soul mate? It was as though we knew each other instantly even though we were complete strangers in this lifetime. I had never experienced anything like it before.

We initially met via a dating app. Being the very jaded NYC dater that I was at the time, I actually contemplated canceling our first date. I wasn't in the mood for yet another "interview" or awkward encounter. "But," I reminded myself as I struggled to get my butt off the couch on a hot Sunday afternoon, "you have to kiss many frogs . . ."

Our date lasted eight hours. After coffee, we strolled through Central Park; then, after sitting and talking on a park bench until dark, we decided to go eat. After dinner, he walked me out to catch a cab heading across town. As we hit the corner of Eighty-Sixth and Central Park West, he sheepishly said something to the effect of: "There was one thing you mentioned on your dating profile that I wanted to ask you about. You said that you were psychic. That was a joke, right?"

I was kind of surprised that it took him eight hours to ask about it. My profile clearly stated that I am a psychic, and his profile clearly stated that he was looking for a God-fearing Christian woman. I remembered reading that, but for whatever reason I'd ignored that blatant sign and swiped right. He, on the other hand, had one of his friends swipe for him and therefore didn't see that critical piece of information until we matched—yet he still initiated the conversation and asked me out.

So no, that wasn't a joke, and his reaction wasn't either—I could feel how disappointed he was, since for him my psychic abilities immediately disqualified me as a potential long-term partner. I could also feel how torn he was. We spent another two hours comparing and contrasting our belief systems while sitting by the side of the road.

While we had similar views on how to conduct ourselves in the world, the fact that I channel Spirit scared him. "It's not possible to discern energies," he said more than once, "since there is only God." This one-and-only god of the Bible communicates with and through us, he believed, meaning any other energies were evil.

I, on the other hand, believe that all of us are psychic, and that my date was no different. He told me about doing automatic writing, having premonitions, and seeing signs everywhere, which seemed to me like channeling, but he defined it within the confines of the Bible and his Christian beliefs.

Even though date number one laid out everything we needed to know about our compatibility, our curiosity about our soul connection prompted us to meet again and again. Each time, our conversation went deeper and allowed me the chance to articulate my belief system and my energetic skills with someone who was knowledgeable and steadfast in his own beliefs. He often talked in metaphors and parables, and he explained his soul's pull, saying, "Imagine I have a certain budget to buy a car that needs to meet a number of my basic needs—like, it has to be practical and functional. Of course, I would rather have a sexy Porsche that really lights me up, but it is just not practical for the life I want to live. In this scenario, you are the Porsche, but what I am looking for is a minivan—a wife that fits the Christian lifestyle I choose to live."

After this brief romance, we decided to call it quits. It hurt. A lot. As they say, "When the student is ready, the teacher will appear." This man came into my life to teach me about staying strong in my conviction, to stay in my true power as a powerful, sexy W.I.T.C.H., no matter how difficult, no matter what I might have to sacrifice in order to do so. I could no more return to a life within the confines of patriarchal gender roles or religious norms than fly naked on a broomstick, cackling at the moon. He surely got one thing right—I most certainly am not a minivan.

When we realize the importance and divine purpose of relationships, it becomes a little easier to gain perspective and allow people to enter and leave our lives in a natural ebb and flow.

Throughout our relationships we also learn to set boundaries that will protect our emotional and spiritual well-being, boundaries that allow us to love some from a distance, let others go, and invite those relationships that support our growth to stay. This is not something that we learn overnight, especially if we have spent our entire lives ignoring our boundaries to please others.

However, the more conscious we become, the more we realize that someone else's emotional well-being isn't more important than our own, and the easier it is to come back to our own center and make decisions in line with our needs. In some instances, we can simply say *no* to things that we don't want to do or that don't make us feel good. In other instances, as in a toxic relationship, a simple *no* isn't going to do the trick, and we will have to walk away.

The journey of becoming a Woman in Total Conscious Healing will inevitably challenge us to use our voices and stand in our power, to remember to put our own emotional and spiritual well-being at the center of our lives. Despite our different experiences, traumas, and triggers, our different belief systems and conditioning, each of us will meet people along the path who are our teachers, healers, lovers, and friends. Accommodating differences is paramount, but even more important is our ability to discern how external relationships are affecting our own power. Always be sure to ask yourself whether a relationship is draining power from you or you are drawing power from the relationship. If you are compromising yourself or your well-being in any way to maintain a relationship, then you are likely not in your full power. A friend of mine beautifully reminds herself of this dynamic by envisioning healthy relationships as an infinity symbol—a mutual and constant relationship of giving and receiving, talking and listening, asserting and surrendering.

YOUR COVEN

For a long time, most of my psychic friends didn't know that I was an Olympian, and nobody really cared about what I did for work. During workshops, we shared information from our higher selves, spirit guides, and spirit loved ones. We each exposed our soul's journey, our core wounds, and the lessons that we are here to learn in this lifetime. These relationships immediately cut past the superficial to the essence of soul. The more I allowed my limiting thoughts and beliefs about the world and myself to dissolve, the more I was able to see others for who they were, where they were in their journeys, and how we could be of service to one another. This level of sharing was raw, honest, and vulnerable.

All relationships are important for our growth. However, some relationships are soul connections that turn into deep, meaningful friendships. This is your *coven*, a collection of people who have heeded the call, who accept your truth, no matter where you are on your journey. Not everyone in your coven has to have the same belief system. What matters is that they understand we all evolve at a different pace and that everyone has their own set of challenges to overcome. Your coven doesn't try to fix you but calls you on your BS, asks you to step up to your potential, holds space for your growth and desires, celebrates your wins, and cheers you on.

Before I could attract like-minded women into my life, I had to become more self-aware and honest, have the courage to follow my heart, and allow myself to speak my truth. Today, my coven is made up of strong, smart, beautiful, deeply flawed, authentic, sexual, witchy, fun, and loving women. Some I met at psychic-development classes, where energetic gifts are normalized and I felt a sense of belonging; others I met during my most vulnerable times, when my truths and insecurities were laid bare; and a few more have found their way into my coven because our paths were destined to cross in this lifetime.

For example, I met my friend Vicki in graduate school. We didn't hit it off until after working on a few group projects together. Both of us were far from having a deep connection with ourselves or each other. As I was going through my years of awakening, Vicki couldn't always understand what was happening, but she would listen and hold space for me to share. Over a decade into our friendship, Vicki began her own awakening, which she was able to recognize because she'd been there for me.

Today, our communities aren't necessarily defined by

a physical space, which is all the more reason why we must intentionally create our coven, a female community that we can rely upon. There is scientific evidence that women process stress or stressful situations by leaning on their social support system. There is research that actually points to the fact that friendships—the relationships we consciously choose—become even more important for our health and happiness as we age, even more than our family relationships, although friendships can be harder to maintain over a lifetime. The simple act of giving or receiving care and participating in nurturing behavior releases oxytocin, a stress-reducing hormone. Therefore, research suggests that strong nurturing relationships between women have a great impact on their overall health and happiness.

Female friendships have the power to heal.

Healing friendships require a level of deep connection—first with the self and then with others. Accepting our own complexities allows us to accept the complexities of others. Your coven knows you, sees you, and understands you for who you are in this moment and holds space for who you are becoming—not blinded by judgments about who you were in the past or who you ought to be in the future. As Women in Total Conscious Healing, we are building a sisterhood with an understanding of the power of women in community, women who are working to fiercely and unapologetically embrace all parts of themselves, who are taking personal responsibility for their own healing, who are committed to contributing to generational healing of the collective, for people of all genders. For everyone. We are a coven of witches.

TRY THIS: FINDING YOUR COVEN

You may be thinking, "I have a lot of friends, but how do I know who belongs in my *coven*?"

There are only a few steps you need to take to figure out who belongs in your coven.

STEP 1:

Become more truthful and authentic about who you are and be courageous enough to share yourself with others.

This will automatically weed out some people who don't like or don't agree with your truth.

STEP 2:

Be discerning and use your conscious awareness about who gets to have access to you in what way.

Your truth, your vulnerabilities, and your inner world are your most valuable assets—your gold. When investing in actual gold, you wouldn't go and give it to just any financial adviser or asset manager without doing your due diligence first. It also wouldn't be smart to invest everything in one place and never make any returns.

The same goes for your inner gold. Give people a little bit at a time and observe how they take care of your most valuable asset. How trustworthy are they? How compassionate and respectful are they? How much do they value your inner gold? Most importantly, how much of their inner gold are they willing to invest in return? How much do they trust in you to take care of their inner gold?

STEP 3:

Remember the infinity symbol—a mutual and constant relationship of giving and receiving, talking and listening, asserting and surrendering.

Once you've established that someone can be a part of your

coven, ask them how they would like you to show up in their life and tell them the same. Be open and honest about your needs and your boundaries to foster that mutually supportive and nurturing relationship.

Practice this, and I promise you that you will find your coven.

REFLECTION

- In what areas of your life do you still feel trapped by the conditioning of your tribal thinking?
- What are some things you can do to broaden your perspective so you can become more conscious?
- What community gatherings do you feel most at home in?
- Are you actively searching for people and communities that align with your view of the world or your passions?
- Are there people in your life whom you need to let go or love from a distance? What steps can you take to make room for the people who add to your growth?
- Identify the people in your life who are part of your coven. What role do they play in your life, and what role do you play in theirs? What are the beliefs, values, or passions that you bond over?
- Don't feel you have a coven? What are some steps you could take to create one? Start by creating a list of qualities you are looking for in people whom you would like to surround yourself with.

CHAPTER 6

SENSUALITY AS A WITCHY ACT

When I was about fourteen or fifteen years old, in the thick of teenage awkwardness, my beloved Libra grandmother visited from Scotland. She bought me a gorgeous tan-colored suede miniskirt, soft to the touch and oh-so-grown-up. The style, and the fact that it came from her, made me feel confident and beautiful.

I wore it on a chilly early-winter day, paired with skin-colored tights, a turtleneck sweater, and a winter coat. After school, I was walking home from the bus stop when my father drove past on his way home from work. The next day, my mother told me that my father had said that it looked like I was naked beneath my coat. What she didn't say—what she didn't need to say—was that I'd done something shameful, dirty even, by not being hypervigilant about my appearance. How foolish was it for me to wear a beige skirt, this kind gift from my beloved grandmother, without first debating whether it would make me look naked and all that that would imply? How foolish was I to not have somehow predicted how I might be judged?

I still get angry when I think about this interaction. I'm not mad at anyone in particular. My parents and the other adults in my life did the best they could with what they knew. They, too, lived within the confines of the same conditioning. In some cases, this looked like privilege; in others, it looked more like risk aversion and restriction. The message was clear: It was my responsibility to monitor the kind of attention I got by the way I dressed and conducted myself. I needed to protect myself from men, and I shouldn't have been "asking for it."

Looking back, I simply cannot remember a single person from my childhood who openly embodied healthy sexuality, or even someone who seemed to comfortably inhabit their own body. Possibly I was too stuck in my own shame cycle to even recognize it. This had nothing to do with Catholicism; in fact, religion didn't really factor into my sexual education much. I was never overtly told that premarital sex was a sin, and we weren't shielded from sex or nudity on TV or in the media in the way that more prudish Americans are. We just didn't talk about it.

We didn't talk about our female bodies and our bleeding, beyond how to dress for our body type and the vaguely ominous "That's what happens when you become a woman" and "We just have to get on with it." Then there were the more obvious warnings around entering womanhood, like "Don't give anybody a reason to talk about you" or, even worse: "You don't want to be one of those girls that is just passed around." When I got my first bleed (and yes, I am purposefully using the word *bleed* here instead of the more palatable terms *period* or *menstruation*), my mother handed me a pad and asked if I knew what it meant. Quickly, with my face turning crimson and my gaze glued to the floor, I answered, "Yes, I know everything." By "everything," I meant whatever I learned from reading *Bravo*, a popular teen magazine in Germany, or what I heard from other girls my age. I felt embarrassed and uncomfortable.

She then instructed me about the disposal of sanitary products and the importance of staying clean and scent-free. We certainly didn't talk about our "stuff" in front of my dad and brother. We certainly didn't discuss the beauty of being a woman within the context of the natural moon phases or the endless cycles of birth, life, death, and rebirth.

In biology class, we learned about functional (reproductive) female anatomy and the process of procreation, but nobody taught us about the size and structure of the clitoris and the eight thousand nerve endings whose sole purpose is arousal and pleasure. Sexual pleasure was not on the curriculum, nor was the lived experience of hormonal changes during the different phases of our monthly cycles. I mean, why would we need to know about all that?

In college, my (male) fencing coach suggested I get on the pill so I wouldn't be inconvenienced by my bleeding during important competitions—or, even better, at all. (Thankfully, I did not comply.) This invasive request of female athletes is quite commonplace in elite sports, and only one of many ways we're penalized because of gender. In the locker-room culture of the athletic community, it was just accepted that during practices and trips to competitions, there were going to be constant sexual innuendos, and that female students should expect unwanted advances, not just from male peers but also from coaches and referees. Imagine being a fifteen-year-old with a mouthful of braces and having a referee say, "I am going to make love to you as soon as you turn eighteen."

Even in those moments when I felt disempowered, I was also acutely aware of the unfairness of it all—how, as daughters, we were raised to carry the burden of having to protect ourselves, our image, and our virginity, while sons were pretty much given free rein as long as they didn't get anyone pregnant.

I'd discover later that the culture in corporate boardrooms was all too similar to that in locker rooms. (This is slowly changing—thank goodness for the brave women and allies who've stood up for #MeToo.) In doing so, I began to appreciate why I was raised to have my guard up and to "shrink" physically and sexually. My parents' interventions came from a good place—they wanted to keep me safe. Being able to hold my own, to endure inappropriate behavior and uncomfortable situations, and to ignore advances or play along as "one of the boys" were all skills critical for the real world. I developed a thick skin and stoic exterior—armor—that ultimately contributed to my professional success.

It did not keep me safe emotionally or spiritually.

I started to examine and unpack these experiences when I was in my late twenties. I was a workaholic with body-image issues, successful yet unhappy and unfulfilled. I lived up to expectations around being "good," even had a false sense of pride in my "goodness," yet felt suffocated and numb. Why did I never feel like an equal? Or, worse, why did I feel like a failure for "giving in" during sexual encounters? Why was I so disconnected from my body, my sexuality, my feminine essence?

REPRESSION

The Great Goddess has been worshipped since Neolithic times (roughly 7000 BCE), and it was women who carried out her rituals. High priestesses lived in temples or sanctuaries and served the spiritual needs of their communities. With the high esteem granted these spiritual leaders and worship of the Divine feminine came the celebration of female bodies, sensuality, and sexual energy. Virginity represented the maiden goddess. A virgin was a woman who was whole unto herself—a woman who didn't need to be married or abstinent, a woman who wasn't owned but was sovereign.

Well, then men took over. With the rise of patriarchal religions and societies, women slipped in status. A new morality, like (female) virginity until marriage, was embraced. (Female) sexuality was seen as dangerous, something to be contained, idealized, and used for the entertainment of men and for procreation. (Female) virginity was used as a weapon against those women who gave in to their sensual pleasures, or those who refused to diminish themselves or play nice.

A few thousand years in, and shame, guilt, and violently enforced conformity continue to keep women in subservient roles. Those who dare to step out of cisgender heteronormativity do so at their own peril. No matter what we do, it seems, we are doing it wrong: If we dress too sexy, then we are "asking for it." If we explore our sexuality freely, then we are sluts. If we are outspoken, then we are bitches. If we are in tune with our psychic energies, then we are witches. Sound familiar?

We are taught to plug and pad ourselves and soldier on with the meeting, the competition, the daily hustle, cramps and all—and please don't complain, be in a bad mood, or be in any way unladylike; be tough, but not too tough if you want a seat at the table. We are told what to look like, how we should dress, how to behave, how to be safe and successful in a man's world, all while being bombarded with unrealistic sexualized imagery. The power of female sexual energy is maligned while simultaneously used to keep us in check. The seductress archetype is weaponized to sell us products with the promise of evoking magnetism—which, if obtained, will be another thing for which we should feel afraid or ashamed. Sex sells just as well as shame does, and put the two together? You've got a few billion-dollar industries.

Even getting basic information or medical care can be a trial. Dr. Elinor Cleghorn, author of *Unwell Women: Misdiagnosis and Myth in a Man-Made World*, notes that the mythologization of women's cycles prevented any scientific understanding of them. This scientific lag, the knowledge gap between what we know about women's bodies and what we know about men's bodies, still exists today. Health-care bias about minorities and underrepresented or marginalized communities is real. With the reversal of *Roe v. Wade*, we are undoing a half century of advancements, ending the right to abortion, limiting access to lifesaving medical treatments, and also calling many fertility treatments into question. Layer on top of that the abstinence-only education that is still being taught in nearly half of US states, further disempowering us and greatly limiting our ability to advocate for our own sexual and reproductive health. The hard-won rights of LGBTQ Americans are also in jeopardy. The "Don't Say Gay" bill, signed into law in early 2022, bans any discussion of sexual orientation or gender identity in early education; apparently, it is inappropriate to talk about reality or to tell younger kids that they can be whatever they want to be. The list goes on and on.

No wonder we learn to disconnect from ourselves, our bodies and emotions and senses.

Sexuality is a natural and fundamental aspect of our human existence, yet it is also the most charged, censored, commodified, and judged. For goodness' sake, the majority of us want it and do it, and we all wouldn't be here without it. And yet we continue to maintain its taboo status. As author, YouTuber, and founder of the Headway Foundation Teal Swan notes, we cannot condemn sex without also condemning our sexual selves and those of others. As long as we continue to do so, it is unlikely that sex and sexuality will become a healthy part of society.

So many of us have experienced some form of sexual trauma and find it difficult to feel safe in our own bodies. So many of us survive by disassociating from our bodies and our sexuality. Many of us have good reason to be afraid, to disconnect, as survivors of sexual trauma. (If this sounds like you, then I would recommend finding a therapist or practitioner you trust to help you, if you haven't already.) Even if you were not violated in this lifetime, at the soul level we remember being persecuted for living in accordance with our true nature. Fear, thought forms, and behavioral patterns have been handed down for generations and now sit deep within the collective female psyche.

We can reclaim our innate power by connecting with our bodies and fighting against outside forces that try to intimidate us into submission and conformity. We can educate ourselves, our daughters, and our communities about our bodies. We can sit in community with other women, to celebrate worshipping Mother Nature and the moon and teach one another about our magic. We can embrace our primal sensual powers through a dedicated self-pleasure practice.

We are whole unto ourselves.

We, as Women in Total Conscious Healing, are called to explore pleasure, life's greatest gift, and let life-force energy move to expand our creative and intuitive abilities, our connection to the Divine feminine. Seriously. Because what is a life without pleasure? What is life without feeling safe in our bodies?

SPIRITUALITY AND SEXUALITY

As I grew my coven and began my own period of sexual expansion, I couldn't help but wonder why, even in spiritualism, we don't really talk about sex and sensuality as part of our spiritual evolution. Individual healing and its impact on the community, yes. Accessing our intuitive and psychic gifts; living by intuitive guidance; building relationships with spiritual guides; regressing through hypnotherapy to learn about past lives; accessing the Akashic records (basically the Universe's database of all events, memories, thoughts, feelings, intents, etc.); channeling wisdom through spoken or written word, song, and dance; and using healing practices such as Reiki to restore balance to our physical and emotional bodies and our chakras—yes. Healing our sexuality wounds, not so much. Though, technically, we are no longer bound by Christian dogma, we still live in a Judeo-Christian society built on a Puritan value system and are still collectively repressed due to cultural conditioning. Most of us still feel awkward or unsafe talking about sex or expressing our sexuality freely.

We have to do better and not simply teach spiritual principles as theory, elevate the intellect above all else, and reproduce the disembodied functioning required for desk jobs and screen time in our spiritual lives. Spiritual, yogic, and tantric teachings recognize the body as inseparable from the mind and spirit, and, in my opinion, these types of embodied practices should be a cornerstone of every spiritual or religious community. The chakra systems, too, provide an excellent model for understanding how the mind/body/spirit functions as a whole.

There are many different chakra systems in the tantric tradition. The six-plus-one chakra system that has become widely known in the West originated in 1577 and was written in Sanskrit in the tradition of the early Vedic texts by Pūrṇānanda Yati. It was translated into English a hundred years ago, in 1918. Chakra comes from the Sanskrit word *cakra*, meaning "wheel" or "circle," and describes subtle energy centers or vortices that are located along our spine. These energy centers are traditionally visualized as spinning disks or lotus flowers. There are a few energy centers that are common in all chakra systems—the sexual center in the lower belly, the heart center, and the crown of the head.

Imperative for our sexual expansion is the second or sacral chakra, located just below the belly button. It is the center of your personal power, sensuality, and creativity, the center through which you create your life and connect, engage, and cocreate with others and the world itself. It is the basis for your identity as a human.

Before we can move out of our day-to-day survival mode into pleasure, creativity, and enjoyment mode, we must address the root chakra, located below the second chakra at the base of the spine. It is primarily concerned with our most basic physical and nonphysical needs of survival, security, and stability as well as connection and belonging. Just like in Maslow's hierarchy of needs, we cannot grow or evolve if these needs aren't met, because we won't be able to focus our attention or energy elsewhere. Since most of us humans on this earthly journey did not have formative years that fostered deep-rooted self-respect, a sense of safety and belonging, and acceptance, we learned to go against our natural desires and instincts, either restricting ourselves, giving in, or overcompensating.

When we give our personal power away and feel unsafe in the world and in our bodies, our sacral chakra is out of alignment, and we lose touch with our passion, with what drives us to experience life to the fullest. The sacral chakra is referred to as our birth canal, and, in a literal sense, this energy center is both the home of our sexual encounters and the place for creation of another being. In a metaphorical sense, it also is where we birth new ideas and the life that we desire. Since there is no real difference between sexual and personal creative energy, when we feel shame for our sexual desires and fear living out our sensual pleasures, we also diminish our ability to be creative and abort new ideas before they can be birthed. When we repress our sexual or creative energy, we lose our imagination, passion, and joy for life, and when we replace those with fear and external expectations, we lose the basis of our true identity. However, when our sacral chakra is in balance, we are able to relish in all the pleasurable things life has to offer, without overdoing or misusing.

By healing your trauma, limiting beliefs, and damaging behavioral patterns, allowing your root chakra to open, you can move forward in life with more confidence and start to feel a sense of safety and belonging in the world. It is then that the serpent energy, or kundalini, can move up your spine and enter your sacral chakra. How much you are able to healthily and safely embody and express your sacred sensuality is directly correlated to how much you are open to receiving in life, in abundance, pleasure, and love.

Sex can be a powerful and sacred form of self-expression and an avenue for physical, emotional, and spiritual expansion and healing.

If you are a Woman in Total Conscious Healing and are still resistant to a healthy expression of your own sensuality and sexuality, then you are likely harboring outdated thoughts and beliefs. I urge you to make mastering your own sexuality a practice—a personal practice (it does not have to include another person or even sexual activity). You are a sexual being, and you deserve to explore your erotic and sensual energy without shame. You deserve to want, to desire, and to allow those desires to be met without restriction. It is your birthright to experience sensations of ecstasy and elevated states of consciousness through your pussy, your portal to the Divine.

EMBRACING THE BODY

Shame is the lie someone told you about yourself.
—Attributed to Anaïs Nin

As I entered my early thirties, I started to become interested in examining the shame, guilt, disgust, fear, and confusion I'd carried in my body for so many years. I started to become interested in conscious and energetic expansion, particularly in how my relationship to my own sensuality and sexuality affects my authentic self-expression, my ability to stand in my own power, my openness to receiving and connecting in healthy relationships, and the creation of the life I want to live. Embracing sensuality and sexuality at a primal level is both a physical experience and an exercise of consciousness.

This has been a gradual evolution for me. When I left behind my studies and athletic career in 2011 and moved five hundred miles east, I was in a place and time in which I was completely starting over—new city, new job, new interests and friends. I had an opportunity to uncover who I wanted to be and not simply fulfill what others expected of me.

New York provided a sense of anonymity that allowed me to feel comfortable slipping into new roles without fear of being found out to be "bad." I spent the first few years working hard and playing hard—when I wasn't traveling for work, exercising, or taking spiritual courses, I was socializing, drinking, dating, partying, and having the occasional casual sexual encounter. I had no real desire to be in a committed relationship, because I had finally given myself some space to unpack and rediscover myself. It was the time of my Saturn return.

In the fall of 2016, three years after my first psychic reading and first contact with the Spiritualist Church, I met a man who was not at all my type. He was fifteen years older than me, a widower, shorter and smaller than me. Yet I was intensely attracted to him, and soon enough I was in love because, above all else, he was kind, attentive, and generous. I was able to break past the limits of physical attraction and learn that emotional and spiritual attraction transcends physicality. For six months, I explored my conditioning: what I thought a relationship and a partner should look like, what an appropriate sexual partner for me was, what great sex even was. A great lover doesn't always come in the "tall, dark, and handsome" package. As my programming around "the right partner" dissolved, I was also healing my expectations around who I had to be in partnership and sexual encounters—someone smaller, daintier, and skinnier. This was the beginning of my conscious sexual expansion.

A few months after we went our separate ways, my dear friend and fellow W.I.T.C.H. Renee invited me to go to the Slipper Room to watch a new group of recent burlesque-school graduates perform for the first time in front of a live audience. I had no clue what to expect. It was an intimate and charming setting with a grandpa's-library vibe—dark wood flooring, wood paneling at the bar, brass ceiling tiles, and outdated wallpaper. The main room was filled with no more than a dozen small round tables facing the elevated stage, and the high ceilings were flanked by mezzanine balcony seating providing a bird's-eye view. The red curtain, adorned with playful and flirty gold fringe, was drawn. Music was playing in the background as we entered the space. I grabbed a drink and took a seat.

I was aware of my own tendency to judge bodies, particularly those of women, and how this stemmed from my own experience of being judged. As an athlete, I was judged in an obvious way—by winning or losing. I trained hard; I was meticulous about my diet and lifestyle. I treated my body like a naughty child that needed to be disciplined for her own good. For the most part, the feedback was positive, in that I had a body that could be made into elite shape and I'd won my way to the very top. Now, however, that mindset wasn't all that helpful. Even though I was no longer an elite athlete, I still fell into the habit of using excessive exercise or food restriction as tools to feel "good" in my body, to gain an illusionary sense of control and even a sense of safety. I still sucked in my stomach.

On top of that was the judgment about appearance

ingrained in us women practically from birth. I still struggled with the deep-seated belief that if I didn't look a certain way, that if I gained weight or my body changed, I would not be lovable. A part of me still believed that if I didn't look like those size 0 models airbrushed in magazines and filtered on social media, I would not be lovable. If I had a zit or a stretch mark or a sunspot or some cellulite, I would not be lovable.

The lights flashed, and the show began. There, onstage, women of all shapes, sizes, and colors strutted their stuff. They shimmied their asymmetrical breasts, jiggled their jiggly butts, fluffed their fluffy hair, swiveled their bony hips, rolled their rounded bellies, flashed great expanses of imperfect skin, reveled in their physicality, flaws and all. They flaunted their costumes and flirted with the audience; they were cheeky, sensual, playful, and enjoying every minute of it. I sat there, absolutely riveted. To witness other women unabashedly adoring themselves, tapping into their sensuality, and courageously using their bodies to make art was so profoundly empowering. *When the student is ready . . .* These women taught me so much in that single performance. This experience made me realize how far I had come, but also how much I had to learn.

After that, I vowed to be more mindful of the ways in which I looked at myself and other women. Awareness is always the first step to healing our wounds. I knew, intellectually, that when we judge others, we're usually just projecting our own insecurities. I had spent a lifetime incessantly comparing myself to others, judging and criticizing how other women displayed their bodies—the size of their butts, the shade of lipstick they'd chosen, the color of their hair, the length of their skirts—all in the hope that somehow this would reflect on me, that it would prove I was pretty enough, skinny enough, sexy enough—lovable enough. (It doesn't make sense, does it?)

Having a newfound and deep admiration for female bodies

and what they are capable of, for their inherent beauty and ability to create life and magic, made the cellulite on my ass seem so irrelevant.

Why, I asked myself, *and for whom are we trying to be skinny and flawless?* We all know that models, influencers, and porn stars aren't the norm, that plastic surgery and airbrushing and extreme diets and the genetic lottery are required for them to look the way they do. Most women have bodies that dimple and jiggle and wrinkle and do all kinds of miraculous feats every single day. What if we defined beauty for ourselves? What if we prioritized how it feels to live in a body, rather than how our bodies look? What if we ate well and exercised because it makes us feel strong and healthy? What if we honored this one vessel we occupy for the entirety of our lives? What if we became aware that our bodies are our channel to the Divine? What if we realized that we *can* love ourselves, that lovability isn't about a few extra pounds or butt shape but an inherent part of being alive?

What if we stopped sucking in our stomachs?

After four years of serious contemplation, countless nudges, and a growing curiosity, I sat with ayahuasca—or Grandmother, as the medicine is fondly called—for the first time. Ayahuasca is a psychoactive brew prepared by a shaman, or *curandero*, and traditionally used for spiritual and religious purposes by ancient Amazonian tribes. It was early February 2022, and the ground was covered in snow. I knew that I had laid the groundwork with my healing, and I was ready to meet Aya and to sit with whatever she had to show me, to be humble and open with no expectations. I couldn't have dreamed up what I experienced if I tried—the physical sensations, the emotional roller coaster, the visions and downloads.

I was lying on my foam mattress in the middle of the ceremony room directly under a skylight. It was night, and the waxing moon illuminated the otherwise dark room. I started to feel the medicine's effects and drifted into a dreamlike state, going in and out of my body, very gently and subtly at first. A ball of pain the size of a ripe watermelon gathered in my lower abdomen, or so I thought. Out of reflex, I put my hands there, but to my surprise the pain was actually located outside my physical body, in my energetic body. As wild and mind-blowing as this realization was, I then realized that the pain wasn't mine. It was energy I had taken on through conditioning, programming, and experience, and, with the help of the shaman, I was able to release and purge it from my body. It didn't end there. I then had a very clear download that Aya was working with the moon to activate and expand my womb space as a portal so I could transmute my pain, the pain handed down over generations in my family and the pain of the collective, and make room to birth and release my creative lifeforce energy into this world. I have never given birth before, but this activation felt like birthing pains—a slow buildup of pain to a full-on contraction and release—over and over again. Expanding and releasing the tension, the pain, the trauma that my sucked-in stomach kept contained. Many associate a purge or a birth with an emptiness, but in reality the space that is created through this process is for expansion, a space to invite in new energy.

A huge lesson for me was that the love and acceptance I was craving came first and foremost from myself. I could learn to sit with the voice that tells me I'm lazy, a failure who does not deserve love. I could learn to feel safe in my body, to feel love in this corporeal home. I could learn to take my power back and release what isn't mine.

Once I could give that to myself, then I could truly open to receive love and acceptance from others. And, just as importantly, I could truly give love and acceptance to others. Because that's what we all want—to feel loved and safe and accepted for who we are, jiggle and all.

TRY THIS: LOVE THYSELF

OPTION 1:

Take back your power and learn to love your body by choosing one thing you love about your body every day. It can be something you love about your appearance, about what your body does for you, about the experiences and sensations your body gives you every single day. For example:

I love that I can see the beauty of the world.

Thank God(ess) for my ability to walk and be active.

Thank God(ess) for my thick, curly hair.

Say affirming statements out loud to yourself, or find an accountability buddy whom you can text these to. With consistency, you will reprogram how you think and feel about your body, and with time you will even learn to love it.

OPTION 2:

Connect with your heart and bring about the feeling of unconditional love. If you have issues feeling this, bring to mind a loved one, a child, or a pet, and feel the love you have for them—now feel this toward yourself. Visualize your heart filled with a beautiful soft-pink light and really feel the love for yourself.

Say these affirmations out loud:

I am enough.

I am worthy of love.

I am loved and lovable.

I am love.

SELF-PLEASURE AND EMBODIMENT

Sexual encounters were a big part of my spiritual expansion. Through this exploration, I learned to face my fears and let down my guard, and that it was OK for me to feel pleasure without guilt. I actively took my power back while getting to know my own range of sexuality, developing a sense of sovereignty and empowerment.

I took a year-and-a-half hiatus from partner sex, however, after reading *Pussy: A Reclamation* by Regena Thomashauer (known as Mama Gena) and, in December 2017, attending her School of Womanly Arts weekend at the Javits Center. She spoke so openly and freely about reclaiming our birthright of a pleasure- and joy-filled life, asserting that self-pleasure must be a deliberate practice. Self-pleasure isn't simply about masturbation and orgasm, although that is a very important aspect of it; it's about identifying what a "turned-on" life looks like and embracing that.

Through abstinence, I learned to differentiate between my basic needs and my desires, how to experience pleasure and being turned on in day-to-day mundane activities like sipping a morning cup of coffee, lighting a candle, washing the dishes, holding the door for someone, going for a leisurely stroll, picking up groceries, eating a delicious peach, wrapping up in a cozy blanket. I learned that, for me, being turned on means adorning my body with lingerie and jewelry—not for a partner but for myself. I learned to flirt for the sake of flirting, to have solo dates and go on solo trips, to cook myself a delicious meal, to get my hair blown out, to dance naked in my living room, to find moments of complete stillness in meditation and prayer, and to buy myself flowers and expensive chocolates. I learned about the powerful energetic response I receive from the Universe when I embody and evoke my own pussy-power.

In this world, it's so easy to prioritize obligations and work over pleasure and rest. It's easy to wait for "when I have a house" or "when I have a boyfriend" or "when everything in my life is perfectly aligned" to live a fully turned-on, pleasure-filled life. It's easy to get caught up in the hustle and masculine stoicism. But the more we are able to pleasure ourselves, the more we dance and pamper and relax and eat chocolate, the more we are able to give and receive from this place. No, it's not selfish or egotistical; it is essential. Plus, ultimately, everyone in your life benefits from this elevated vibration and consciousness.

As Women in Total Conscious Healing, we decide to treat ourselves how we expect others to treat us. We know that we don't have to wait for someone's permission or generosity, that it is our own responsibility to identify what we do and do not want and then to open ourselves up to receiving exactly that. We have to internalize our worth and deservedness and set a clear energetic bar. We have to dedicate ourselves to pleasure as a self-care practice.

From my practice, I felt the shift in my body, my energy, and my consciousness—and I began to make sense of what that meant and who I was becoming.

That brought me to internal family systems (IFS) therapy, a psychotherapy modality and paradigm developed by Dr. Richard Schwartz in the early 1980s. This isn't traditional talk therapy but rather a process of acknowledging and getting to know all our internal parts and their roles. Usually, our parts—e.g., fear or rage—take on certain roles to protect ourselves at younger ages and subconsciously influence our behavioral and emotional response when we encounter certain triggers in our daily life. Through a process of bringing compassion and understanding to these parts, we build trust, and in turn these parts reveal often-forgotten memories. IFS therapy helps uncover our true self that exists underneath all our personality components.

IFS gave me access to my younger self at different ages and to all my parts that are actively creating my internal and external reality. I was building a relationship with my inner world, getting to know my inner child at different ages, and understanding my trauma, triggers, and defense mechanisms, yet I still didn't know how to express and integrate them into my external reality. That's when I found embodiment.

Embodiment is the process of bringing awareness to moment-to-moment thoughts, feelings, sensations, and energies in the physical body. It is the process of feeling deeply and fully, even the uncomfortable feelings we would rather fix or avoid, and having all your parts online. It is the practice of less thinking—more feeling, more loving, more being.

There are many different embodiment practices, but at the core they all use a multilayered approach of breath, sound, movement, felt sense, surrender, and intimacy. During feminine embodiment, we use a down-regulating breath that brings us into the present moment and into the body as the foundation. We move our normally shallow, constricted breath all the way from our head to our heart and into our sacral space, activating our life force. As feminine beings, we hold a lot of emotions in the pelvis. Breathing layered with intuitive and fluid movements, like pelvic tilting, allows us to soften and unwind, and brings core wounds, fears, anxiety, blocks, and emotions out of the head and into our bodies. Another critical layer is sound. The throat connects the head with the heart and creates another mind-body connection. We use ancient sounds such as "ha"; we yawn, sigh, growl, yell, and laugh. This is a practice of living in depth and feeling our feelings.

My teacher, Alexandra Roxo, who is a bestselling author, creative, and transformational coach specializing in the intersection of spirituality and sexuality, emotional and creative expression, and embodiment, says that practicing isn't healing, but is necessary for transformation. Our imprints and behavioral, mental, and physical habits have been with us for a very long time, and in a resting position we will default to imprinted thoughts, body posture, and behaviors. It takes practice and devotion to transform those imprints. Embodiment practices help us become aware of sensations and the way of our body. We learn what it feels like to be embodied versus disembodied, to discern what emotions are our own and what is external to us, and to take concepts such as "love" or archetypes out of the abstract and into the physical body. However, it will not help us address underlying trauma and core wounds that undoubtedly will be brought to the forefront the more embodied you become. It is therefore important to supplement with therapies and healing modalities that specialize in trauma and can address deep-seated wounds. For me, the combination of IFS and feminine embodiment have been extremely beneficial.

As children, we are each so in tune with our imagination and able to freely play with expressing ourselves in different ways. As adults, we are taught how to fit a mold. Alexandra considers embodiment artists' work, actors' work, the work of returning to that curious and open childlike state. Embodiment isn't about fixing anything or performing, but about accessing what is already there and inching closer to becoming more fiercely and authentically embodied and expressed, inching closer to your whole and true self.

In the advanced embodiment class, we evoke textures of experience, emotions, and archetypes within ourselves and play with subtleties and extremes so we can familiarize our-selves with and activate our bodies and our nervous systems. All of us are the nurturing mother, the playful child, the psychic witch, the madwoman, the seductress, the creatrix, the virgin, the wisewoman—we all embody these archetypes and more. We don't have to actually be in these roles to experience them. For example, we don't have to physically give birth to embody the textures of being a mother. We can nurture our own inner child and the children of others; we can nurture Mother Earth and our houseplants and our loved ones.

As we practice this full range of expression within a safe container, we begin to see these textures show up more authentically in our day-to-day lives. We express the language of the body, our sensitivity and sensuality. We find our edges and gently push past them.

TRY THIS: EMBODY YOUR FEELINGS

Let's explore how a feeling or felt sense manifests for you. Practice this with any emotion that is present for you right now.

STEP 1:

Take a moment to ground yourself in your body by taking a few deep breaths and putting your hands on your heart and belly. Ask yourself what it is that you are feeling at this moment. Then listen, explore, and stay curious about this part of you.

Am I in my head or in my body?

Am I disembodied in fear? Am I feeling open and connected to my breath?

STEP 2:

For the purposes of this exercise, you might say that you "feel angry."

- Acknowledge this feeling without judgment, without attaching a story to it, and without trying to change or fix it. Simply sit with this emotion and breath. Stay with it and feel it.
- Notice how this feeling shows up for you. Are you clenching your jaw? Tightening your fists? Is your heart beating faster? Does this feeling show up in a particular part of your body? How so (e.g., tingling, heat, constriction, pain)?
- Stay with the emotion and become aware if you are restricting its expression. Are you holding back tears? Are you clenching your jaw in an effort not to scream? Are you staying motionless even though you want to punch and kick or run?
- Take a deep breath and allow yourself to release in whatever way feels natural and intuitive. Don't hold back. Stomp your feet, punch a pillow, sob on the floor. If you are embodying joy, you might giggle like a schoolgirl and dance like an ethereal fairy.

This is the process of transforming a physical sensation into expressed energy—leaving you feeling more embodied, clearheaded, and heart-centered. This might feel difficult and crunchy in the beginning. With time, you will develop a sensitivity to your body's language, and it will be easier to stop judging your feelings, avoiding emotions, and reacting from the story the mind has attached to the feeling, as well as to express intuitively.

RECLAIMING THE SACRED SLUT

The deepest work is usually the darkest.
—Dr. *Clarissa Pinkola Estés*

Eventually, after a period of integration, I moved into a phase where I was more intuitively and consciously guided to people, relationships (casual and committed), encounters, and experiences that pushed my boundaries in a healthy way. Apparently, I was still holding on to certain judgments of what is "acceptable," "good," "normal," and "ladylike" and needed to be shown where those inhibitions were still holding me back, where I was resisting my own expansion.

I was curious, and less afraid of "getting into trouble" because of this curiosity. Eve was curious about the forbidden fruit, tempted by the snake, a symbol of our sensual and creative life force. Well, I had finally tapped into my sensual energy, and I didn't need a snake to tempt me.

I took my first-ever edible on a trip to Israel when I was thirty-four. (This was before my work with ayahuasca.) With the constant drug testing that was part of my athletic career, I'd stayed away from all drugs, except the most widely accepted drug of alcohol, of course. Now, in a Bedouin tent, a friend surprised us with some edibles that she had brought for this occasion. Although nervous, I felt like, if there ever was a moment to pop my pot cherry, it should be underneath a million stars in the Israeli desert.

I said yes. That decision to taste the forbidden fruit was a catalyst, and afterward I started to say yes whenever I felt intuitively guided to do so, when there was a strong *yes* in my body.

I ventured back into the world of partner sex and sensuality. Once I came out from under the fear-based veil that kept me sexually repressed for most of my teens and twenties, only to realize that embracing my sexuality not only set me free but allowed me to tap into my own feminine power, I intuitively knew that I needed to further lift the veil on what is widely considered taboo. I surrendered limitations and expectations of the mind—what a partner or partners should look like, what is appropriate, what is too risqué. What is obscene. Dr. Clarissa Pinkola Estés explains, in her book *Women Who Run with the Wolves: Myths and Stories of the Wild Woman Archetype*, that the origin of the word *obscene* comes from the Hebrew word *ob*, meaning "sorceress" or "wizard." In ancient-goddess cults the word *obscene* was used to mean a kind of sexual/sensual enchantment that causes good emotional feeling. As a Woman in Total Conscious Healing, I went with that and then some.

It was like I was conducting an experiment, with myself as the subject. I explored my body, my desires, my needs, my turn-ons, my kinks, and my boundaries; I flirted, seduced, played, and turned on my sensual energetic powers. I explored and read books about the evolution of sexual behavior, poly-amory, and psychedelics. I continued to get intuitive nudges to go where I'd been afraid to go before, to explore what I thought of as darker, kinkier, drawing-outside-the-lines kinds of sex and sensuality, to explore the sacred slut.

Who is the sacred slut? She is not ashamed of her pleasure and her sexual power. She understands that her sexual energy is the purest form of life-force energy, and that at the core of all desires is to be one with self, with others, with love. She doesn't use her sexual power to manipulate, because her sexuality is a manifestation of Divine consciousness. Her body is a temple, and her sex is a prayer.

For me, this exploration wasn't all magical. Even though I usually found safe spaces in which to explore, I was still op-erating within the wider rape culture of patriarchy, and, un-fortunately, I did experience a few uncomfortable situations. Sadly, like most women I know. Sometimes this had something to do with inebriation; once or twice a person coerced me or made sexual advances that I'd communicated I didn't want. Sometimes I dissociated from my body and my voice. Even though I know these experiences weren't my fault, I continue to deal with a sense of shame and guilt, and I worry that I'll be judged. I can imagine a critic tsk-tsking, shaking their head, and thinking, *You should have just kept your legs shut.*

On the whole, however, embracing my full-body *yes*es led me to beautifully expansive people and experiences. Just as people travel to different countries to learn about different cultures and ways of life, I journeyed through sex to broaden my perspective on sexuality and consciousness. After all, we shouldn't condemn what we do not know.

Just as I intuitively knew that I was ready to take this journey, I also knew when I was done. I felt at peace. I had tapped into shunned parts of myself and had given them an opportunity to be seen, to be embodied, and to play. Now it was time to figure out how I wanted to integrate my new knowledge into my being and how to harness my sacral energy for myself. Breaking the "good girl" conditioning and embracing other archetypal parts within myself—the sacred slut, the Goddess, the wilde woman—is but a stop on the journey to living in full authentic expression. It was time for the next experiment, the next journey toward a full-body *yes.*

TRY THIS: SELF-PLEASURE EXPLORATION

Cultivating our sacral, sexual, and creative energy for the purposes of our own pleasure and self-exploration is a crucial part of taking our power back. Our sacral energies are first and foremost our own, and we must remember that we are whole unto ourselves. It is from this space that we can safely share these energies with others and express in a way that is empowered and aligned. Here are some ideas I adapted from Mama Gena, author of *Pussy: A Reclamation*, and added to for exploring your sacral energy.

STEP 1: DATE YOURSELF!

Take yourself out. Do what you would if you were seeking outside validation. Put on a sexy dress and lingerie, choose a cute date spot, text your girlfriends about this exciting date you have planned. If that doesn't feel right, then ask yourself: "Why would I do certain things and show up in certain ways for someone else, if I'm not willing to show up for myself in that same way? What about going on dates actually feels pleasurable to me?" Do that!

Plan a date night at home. Cook yourself a nice meal and open a nice bottle of wine. Dessert too. Actually set the table. Buy yourself flowers. Wear something that makes you feel good about yourself. After dinner, draw a bath, read a book, listen to music, have a naked dance party in your living room. End the night with sexual pleasure. Do whatever lights you up and brings you into the moment. Give yourself the pleasure you previously waited for others to give to you. Love yourself simply because you deserve it.

STEP 2: BE CREATIVE.

Put on some music and dance, paint, play an instrument, sing, write, make Pinterest boards, cook up a new recipe. Anything that gets the creative juices flowing.

STEP 3: CREATE A SACRED SELF-PLEASURE RITUAL.

Practice getting comfortable in your body, touching your body, looking at your body in the mirror and complimenting yourself. Practice self-massage with some body oil. Light candles, play music, set intentions. Experiment with pleasure tools—try a vibrator or jade egg or crystal wand.

Practice hip-opening movements through intuitive movement, dance, yoga, or stretching.

CALLING IN A CONSCIOUS PARTNER

I had dedicated time and energy to healing through therapy, inner-child work, embodiment practices, breath work, and life experiences. I had cultivated my psychic witchy and goddess energy, stepped way out of my comfort zone, and examined my beliefs about pleasure and deserving relationships.

I now wanted a partnership in which my partner and I were not only committed to each other and the relationship but to personal growth and expansion. Someone who would be my mirror and allow me to be his, for each of us to reveal where we are not showing up in our truest and highest form. We can go a long way toward healing our witch wounds, our traumas, our triggers, and the toxic masculine/feminine by being on our own spiritual journey and by committing to our own spiritual practices. But learning how to relate to one another in a healthy and authentic manner regardless of gender and programming can only really happen in relationships. It is in relationships where we are presented with countless opportunities to recognize and unpack our behavior, our thinking, how we love or withhold love, and even the language we use.

This, for me, has been the hardest work of all.

As with any practice, spiritual or relational practice requires commitment to doing better and to staying open when things get hard, plus a willingness to be uncomfortable and to show up differently. To be able to relate to one another from a place of love and respect, we have to take personal responsibility for how we show up or fail to show up for ourselves and the sacred container of a relationship, be it with a romantic or platonic counterpart or as a caretaker.

A loving, conscious, heterosexual, and monogamous relationship works for me, but it's certainly not for everyone. Love, partnership, and sexuality exist on a spectrum, and everyone should be able to choose what that looks like for them.

Eventually, as you continue on your path of becoming a Woman in Total Conscious Healing, you will remember that you are already powerful. You will remember that it is your birthright to claim your true power by embodying and connecting with your highest and most authentic self. You will remember that this is the most important relationship of all.

March 13, 2020, was the day I was scheduled to have my first consultation to freeze my eggs. For weeks, there had been strange reports about a new kind of flu in China, and it just so happened that this was also the day that the world shut down. COVID-19 spread across the globe, and we all stayed inside and prayed and waited.

In August 2020 an old friend of my sister's reached out to me on Instagram. Matthias and I, both with newfound time on our hands, started chatting, and eventually he admitted that he'd had a crush on me and had even joked with my sister twelve years prior that he would marry me one day. When I went home to Germany for Christmas, we met for the first time in more than a decade. He lived in Heidelberg, which is about a two-hour drive from Eislingen, where I was staying with my parents. Luckily, he was coming to spend Christmas with his father, who lives two towns over.

Every year on Christmas Eve morning, our entire district would come together to celebrate Holy Morning by drinking *Glühwein* and sharing in the holiday spirit. Since COVID put a stop to that, my sister and I decided that we would host our own Holy Morning on my parents' terrace with our family and some neighbors. We cooked up some delicious *Glühwein*; bundled up in our winter coats, hats, and gloves; and stood around a fire that my father had lit.

Matthias had mentioned that he would be coming home on Christmas Eve, so naturally I invited him to stop by. He stood nervously on the terrace and spent most of his visit conversing with my sister; no one in my family knew that we had been talking, and they assumed he'd stopped by to see her. With COVID regulations and a curfew in place, we wouldn't have a chance to go on a more "traditional" date or have much alone time together. To see me again before I flew back to New York on January 2, Matthias cut short his ski vacation in Austria and invited himself to my sister's apartment, where I was staying the night before my flight. I am glad he did. We had a chance to connect more casually and feel our attraction building. We even shared a kiss.

Back in New York, I started FaceTiming with Matthias for hours every day. We both were interested in this thing that was developing between us, but the US borders were closed, so he couldn't come to visit. "I would really like to take you on a date and spend some time getting to know you in person! I would be on the next plane to New York if I could. What if we met somewhere we can both travel to right now?" he suggested one day. "Let's go to Mexico!"

A year into the pandemic, Matthias and I met in Tulum. On my flight to Cancún, I sat on the plane, tears rolling down my face. Not because I was sad, but because I had a deep knowing that my life would change. This felt different and right on time.

At this point, we had been getting to know each other via text and video calls for six months. We'd already had big conversations about our expectations for the future, kids, spiritual views, our non-negotiables, and so on, but we hadn't had the chance to observe each other in day-to-day situations: how we behaved, how we treated other people, and how we would treat each other. We knew we liked each other, we knew we were attracted to each other, and finally we were getting to spend time together in the flesh. It was the missing piece to figure out what was developing between us.

We stayed in a small boutique hotel right on the beach, in a room with a partial ocean view. Matthias insisted that he pick me up from our hotel room for our first official date, and he took me to a lovely seaside restaurant. After dinner and drinks, we strolled along the shore, stopping to hold each other close and dance under the light of the full moon, the ocean waves our music. It was magical. It was perfect. We started our relationship in a very spiritual place, an energy vortex, on a full moon.

After our weeklong trip led to the decision that we would give this relationship a try despite the many obvious hurdles, we continued to date long-distance, meeting up in Germany and Mexico again, and, once vaccines were widely available and borders had reopened, in New York. In October 2021, Matthias asked his company if he could transfer to the United States. He moved to NYC on March 25, 2022, almost exactly a year after our first date in Tulum. Turns out both of us had this deep and strong knowing that we would be together, one way or another.

We had both been single and living by ourselves for many years, so moving in together was a big step. I hadn't lived with a man since growing up with my father and brother. Quickly, I could feel how I was reverting back to the hyperaware and anxious people-pleasing Siobhan that I was when still living at home, being triggered by the slightest of mood changes. I responded by either wanting to fix things from my masculine energy or retreating, fawning, and closing my heart, which in turn triggered Matthias's abandonment wounds. *When the student is ready* . . . I was finally ready to face my wounding and programming in an intimate relationship while cohabitating in a seven-hundred-square-foot apartment on the Upper East Side of Manhattan.

I now needed to learn how to put all that I'd been working on into practice in a relationship: to embody my feelings when I am triggered, stick to my feminine practice to not lose myself in the story of the emotions, find courage to share and express my wounding, draw boundaries from an open heart, and practice meeting my partner's masculine frustrations with my feminine playfulness. This kind of work is only possible when the relationship is a safe container.

Like all relationships, my relationship mirrors back to me when I am acting from my wounding. It is helping me uncover parts of myself that require tending to, like feeling safe to express my full range of emotions or noticing when I revert to my anxious and people-pleasing tendencies. I am learning to sit with honest and loving feedback and to share it just the same. My sexuality is deepening as I become more fully embodied through energetic expansion as part of physical experience.

In a conscious relationship, we become more aware of when and how we close our heart from giving or receiving love. We learn how to keep opening it, over and over again, no matter how scary and vulnerable it feels at times to be in deep connection with another. What makes a conscious relationship as beautiful as it is difficult is that perfectly flawed individuals, each on their own healing and growth journey, allow each other the space and grace to evolve, without abandoning themselves or their partner(s) in the process. This is not Prince(ss) Charming arriving on a white stallion, a teenager playing love songs outside your window on their boom box, a diamond engagement ring in a glass of champagne, a happily-ever-after under a tropical sunset, a white picket fence and a passel of babies. The work is always just beginning.

REFLECTION

- What are your beliefs about sensuality and sexuality? Where did those beliefs originate?
- What are your beliefs about pleasure? Where did those beliefs originate?
- How are you restricting yourself or keeping yourself under control? Where do you deny yourself pleasure and why? What are you not allowing yourself to feel?
- What is keeping you from being able to express yourself creatively?
- Are you in your personal power, personal desire, and personal pleasure in relationship with yourself? In relationship with others?
- Do you feel safe in your body? What is preventing you from feeling safe?
- What would be scary about feeling your personal power or showing it to other people?
- What would happen if you expected people to relate to you?
- Have you felt a sense of lost passion and purpose?
- What would happen if you were open to receiving what you desire most? What is it that you would have to face, admit, give up?
- What does your slutty goddess want?
- Where do you still conform to the "good girl" or "ladylike" roles and expectations? Does it feel restrictive? What could you do to safely explore the obscene, forbidden, or taboo?

CHAPTER 7

REDEFINING SUCCESS, POWER, AND LEGACY

It is quite true what philosophy says: that life must be understood backwards. But then one forgets the other principle: that it must be lived forwards.

—Søren Kierkegaard

Most of us are afraid of our own power and potential. We are afraid of what we are capable of and how life could unfold if we let go of the reins and stepped into our truth, our deepest knowing. We are afraid to meet our edges and to sit with our discomfort. We are afraid to let go of our armor and masks. We are afraid of forging a different path.

When did we start to fear our own power? When did we decide that it was better to play small and be safe than to live fully? When did we decide that acquiring property, possessions, and wealth was the ultimate goal in life? Again, we can look back to the agricultural revolution and the rise of patriarchal, monotheistic religions. The transition from a nomadic hunter-gatherer lifestyle to a location-based agricultural lifestyle during the Neolithic Revolution around twelve thousand years ago allowed people (men) to acquire property and other forms of wealth. People (men) could hold on to the fruits of their labor, and because there were now structures in place, both physical and social, to secure possessions, the tangible goal of accumulation became in vogue. Some people (women, children, slaves, and indentured servants) were considered another type of possession, and so they, too, needed to be safeguarded—in other words, they were also made to fit within those structures. Those who didn't, who wanted to roam free, were punished.

Thousands of years of this, and here we are. Most of us no longer live on farms, but the drive to accumulate has only grown as our basic needs are met and we grow hungry for non-essentials. Would we survive without the latest smartphone, car, exercise bike, designer jeans? Of course. But that would be unpatriotic, anti-capitalist. It is our duty to contribute to the economy by making and buying, making and buying, making and buying. The correct path, the socially approved path, is that which is focused on monetary and material success and power. Our legacy is "the amount of money or property left behind."

And so we were all raised in what I like to call disempowered empowerment. I was raised to be independent, tough, strong, smart, hardworking, disciplined, and persistent—all great masculine qualities that I certainly need to be outwardly successful in this patriarchal world and for which I am grateful. I was also raised to be obedient.

FROM ROLE-SELF TO TRUE SELF

In 2016, my mother was diagnosed with cancer. I heard the news in May, the same month that I graduated from a yearlong psychic-development course.

Of course, this news was the most devastating for my mother, but it profoundly affected all of us. I had planned to be in Germany for my brother's wedding in early July, but after the diagnosis, I arranged to be there for when she started an aggressive combination of chemo and radiation.

I spent a total of six weeks in Germany, balancing working remotely on US hours, accompanying my mother to her appointments, visiting her in the hospital, taking care of my parents' home and dog, and helping with last-minute wedding planning. I also volunteered to take on the role of tour guide for a weeklong trip to Scotland that my mother had planned for twenty of her English students. My mother runs her own tutoring school, and once a year she organizes a trip for her adult students to a location where they can practice their language skills. Since I was already going to be in Europe for my brother's wedding, I had planned to join the trip as a vacation, to explore new parts of Scotland and our heritage. But once my mom fell ill and could no longer lead the trip herself, my sister and I stepped in and took over for her.

One morning during this trip to Scotland, I felt so weak that I could hardly get out of bed. I was completely burned out, with nobody to blame but myself. You might say that taking all this on was the honorable thing to do—I stepped up to help out my family when they needed me. You might wonder if I am mentioning this because I want to be acknowledged for what I did. Maybe so. Whether I did it for honor or acknowledgment, I did it at the expense of my own emotional, spiritual, and physical well-being.

I had been on my spiritual path for about two years at that point, and while my spirituality helped me hold space for my mother, I had completely lapsed into the old, familiar role of people-pleasing, carry-everything-on-my-shoulders daughter. My mom was undergoing treatment while trying to make sense of the question "Why is this happening to me?" and I was trying to keep everything else going so she didn't have to worry. I hadn't learned yet how to care for others without abandoning myself, and I didn't understand yet the absolute necessity of self-care, of setting boundaries and asking for support as an integral part of a spiritual practice. Instead, I filled the vacuum created by my mother's absence, thereby giving others a pass from stepping up. I took on the caretaker role, the selfless-martyr archetype, that my mother had modeled, which ultimately led to her being resentful and ill. I, too, started to feel resentful in that role. Because let's face it— selflessness is not in fact honorable.

Not that I was having these thoughts at the time—I was merely functioning on autopilot and adrenaline. It was in the months (and years) after my return to the US, when my siblings took over my mother's care, that the unpacking and reflecting started. It is very difficult to heal in an environment surrounded by energies and structures that cause us to behave in certain ways, so I had to create some distance first before I could even begin to process what had happened.

I reflected on many things, one being the fact that my mother spent her whole life overworking and overextending herself to meet the needs of others and to prove her worthiness, as a wife, mother, and woman. This role-self that she was living in was trying so hard to meet her needs to be seen, feel acknowledged, and feel in control. Overfunctioning and being overly independent was easier than sitting with her emotions, understanding her needs, and finding ways to have those needs met, by either herself or others.

I believe that unreleased and unacknowledged emotions and trauma will fester and manifest in the body in the form of "dis-ease." As lauded as it is in our society to be selfless and overworked, especially for women, it is not actually honorable.

This was my mother's journey, right on time for her second Saturn return, and I was in a supporting role. Still, I learned a great deal going through that. I was pushed outside my comfort zone, given a new perspective, and shown where I still had work to do. I recognized just how much what we see and experience growing up affects how we show up for others and ourselves. It was a wake-up call. My mother's role-self hadn't served her, and me stepping into that same role wasn't helping anyone, either, but perpetuating outdated gender roles.

In her book *Adult Children of Emotionally Immature Parents: How to Heal from Distant, Rejecting, or Self-Involved Parents,* Lindsay Gibson describes how the conditioning we receive from our family of origin forms our role-self. That which we take on in childhood runs deep, especially as the role-self is meant to get us the love and affection from our parents that we desire. We learn to mistrust our true self, the truth at the center of our being, and our true desires. When people experience a breakdown, emotionally or physically, they often think it is their "self" that is breaking down. But, in reality, it is our struggle to deny our emotional truth that is breaking down. The pain of living in the role-self begins to outweigh any potential benefits, and it becomes more and more difficult to remain emotionally unconscious. Then it is time to rediscover and learn to trust the guidance of our true self.

Our true self, like a healthy child, wants to grow, be known, and express itself. It does so through our intuition and our feelings. Only if we spend our adult years learning to recognize and trust ourselves again, to do the work, can we get closer to our true self. Our conditioning will override our innate wisdom at times, like it did for me when I took over for my mother in 2016. That is a natural part of the process—forgetting and remembering. But the longer we ignore subtle intuitive pings and signs from the Universe, the louder and more severe they'll be. Hence the breakdown. These dark periods can be an opportunity to develop a deeper understanding of and a more intimate relationship with your true self; they can lead to greater self-actualization.

What I learned by observing my mother's own awakening, how my family of origin coped, and how I responded was that self-care wasn't something that any of us knew how to do. I got to observe the roles we were all playing and saw that support and love in our family was directly correlated with the amount of effort and doing. I also learned that awakening to family dynamics can cause guilt and shame to arise, as well as a fear of losing connection when we choose to create boundaries. I was given an opportunity to refocus, to reaffirm who I was and who I am becoming.

I set out to strengthen my connection to my true self, so that the next time—and there will be a next time—I am asked to return to an old, familiar role, I will have a concrete reminder to keep me on course. I call this the conscious healing elixir.

THE CONSCIOUS HEALING ELIXIR

These are the three simple and fundamental questions:

Who am I?

What do I feel?

What do I desire?

WHO AM I?

On the surface, the answer seems pretty obvious. We've answered this question a million times, on résumés and in dating profiles and at parties. *Who am I?* Most of you would give your name, where you live or grew up, your marital status, what you do for work, and any other interesting fact or title that you hold. You would rattle off a combination of a little bit of business and a little bit of fun. But is that really how you identify?

Is this truly who you are? Or is this the box that society has drawn around you?

I had to really sit with this for a long time. The reality was that I heavily identified with the labels that were assigned to me and I derived my value from my achievements and titles. In fact, when I quit fencing, I didn't know who I was. Who am I if I am not this athlete anymore? Who am I when there is nobody to judge me? Who am I when not defined by my achievements, labels, and titles? Who am I if not a sister, a daughter, an athlete, an Olympian, a college grad, a consultant, a businesswoman, a feminist, an immigrant, a psychic, a friend, or a witch?

In order to arrive at a substantive answer, I had to first gain awareness around my conditioning and my ego-driven thoughts, to learn to recognize and start to release the stories and habits that kept me hiding behind this armor of roles and titles. This is an ongoing process of seeing and shedding illusions, layer by layer by layer.

At a party recently, I was introduced as "Siobhan—oh, and by the way, did you know that she is an Olympian?" This was funny and annoying to me at the same time. I would never introduce myself as an Olympian; I rarely mention it, and only if it naturally comes up. I'm certainly proud of my accomplishment, but what does it say about who I am now?

An introduction like that usually says more about the person doing the introducing. It's a title with prestige, and using it is an attempt to elevate my status and qualify my presence at the party. But at this point it holds more weight for strangers or acquaintances than it does for me or my family and friends. If you stripped me of that title tomorrow, I would hardly notice it was gone.

After the party, I described this interaction to a close friend from an intuitive-development class. She laughed. "I didn't know for over a year after meeting you that you were an Olympian," she said. It was irrelevant to a class in which the whole point is stripping off emotional armor and celebrating each student's unique gifts. It's irrelevant to our connection, and it certainly didn't come up in conversation. All our basic backgrounds, our day jobs and alma maters and accolades, revealed themselves as added flavor over time.

We assume roles because we don't know that we have a choice until we go down the path of becoming more intuitively self-aware. You might be thinking that some people truly don't have a choice in terms of the roles they have been assigned or have chosen to step into. What I'm talking about is identity—we always have a choice in how much we *identify* with familial, societal, cultural, and religious expectations associated with those roles.

Nobody can tell you who you are, because only you know what's in your heart.

This is what becoming self-aware is all about. Reidentification means consciously choosing what you stand for and from where you derive your value. It means reidentifying your place within the larger whole; your place in the Universe compared to your hometown, state, country, alma mater, and so on. It means reidentifying as a spiritual being who is walking the earth as a human. It means reidentifying as a Woman in Total Conscious Healing.

Who are we when we strip away all the roles and titles? How do our roles and titles connect with what we believe, what we value, how we behave, and the choices we make? Once we've identified our roles and associated behaviors, then we can identify which fit, which don't, and which parts of our identity aren't even represented on the list. What are the parts that we keep hidden because we think they are too much, too weird, or not acceptable?

Deconditioning and reidentification, getting to know

yourself and reinventing yourself over and over again, aren't done with a simple journaling exercise, although that is a fantastic start. It takes time to figure out what parts of ourselves we are ready to let go of and what parts of our core, our heart, and our shadow we are willing to bring forth and integrate into our being. This is an ongoing process as we move through life and uncover new parts and new roles for ourselves. Be patient, stay curious, and, most of all, be brave.

WHAT DO I FEEL?

Once we tune in to what we feel in our heart and Spirit, our intuition kicks into gear and starts to communicate with us in so many delightful ways.
—Sonia Choquette

For me, getting in touch with my feelings has been way harder than identifying the roles I have taken on. At the beginning of my journey, I honestly didn't even know how to describe or name what I was feeling at times. I had spent most of my life living from logic and the mind, in a state of disassociation from my body. It was only during fencing that I was able to embody and release pent-up stress, tension, frustration, anger, joy, and excitement even—and no better way than to release screams and growls after hitting someone with a sword.

Softening—through dark nights of the soul, medicine ceremonies, healing in relationships, therapy, surrendering, and relaxing through humor and ease—made me aware of how tightly I constrict myself. I had spent an incredible amount of energy sucking in my belly, I realized, trying to obtain the modern ideal of a flat stomach. In doing so, I constricted my musculature and my breath, sacrificing free flow through and sensation within this power center. I cut myself off from my gut—the physical gut and the energetic or intuitive gut. I cut myself off from the joy, pleasure, and magic that is possible within and through this body I am living in.

We dismiss our body's natural intelligence when we ignore bodily functions such as hunger, our need to release ourselves, our need for rest when we bleed. We hold the urge to go to the restroom just to finish that last email or Netflix series. We ignore hunger pangs or drops in energy in order to stay small, "lovable," and "healthy." We wear tight clothing that restricts breathing and circulation to avoid the appearance of jiggles and dimples and bloating and, God forbid, panty lines. We pay thousands of dollars and submit ourselves to elective pain to laser away freckles, hair, or sunspots that make us uniquely beautiful. We restrict ourselves from freely expressing our emotions to avoid being labeled "hysterical," "too emotional," "unfucked."

I realized that I needed to get out of my head, to learn how to drop into my body, and to not just make sense of my feelings but to embody them. Boy, did I have my work cut out for me. Still do.

I simply couldn't logic my way out.

I really had to learn to sit with my feelings and process, to drop into my body through meditation, visualization, breath work, and other embodiment practices, as well as therapy. I'd ask myself: *What is it I'm feeling? Where is it located in my body? Do I recognize this feeling from a previous experience? Is it expansive or constricting? Does the feeling have a color? What is this feeling trying to tell me? What is it that I need?*

When I first started internal family systems therapy, I practiced tuning in to my body, listening, and observing. I could feel a sense of restriction behind my heart and all the way up through my throat, but I couldn't for the life of me name the feeling associated with the sensation. This was its own separate frustration, this inability to name it after all the work I'd done to bring awareness to feelings, to try to name them, and to practice releasing them through embodiment. This was new, and I had no word for it. After isolating and making friends with all the different sensations present, I realized that what I was feeling was a combination of a few different feelings—judgment, embarrassment, and fear. Our emotional body is complex, and learning what we feel is a continuous adventure into our internal world.

The more I become an active observer of my feeling body, especially during difficult times, such as my Saturn return or dark nights of the soul, the more I am able to recognize what my feelings and the sensations in my body are trying to communicate to me. I am also continuing to strengthen my intuition and my psychic abilities. I am learning that I can get answers to my fundamental questions of *Who am I? What do I feel? What do I desire?* by going within and learning to trust that I have an intuitive knowing that will guide me.

As a Woman in Total Conscious Healing, do you pay attention to your feelings? Do you stop and take the time to drop into your feelings, or do you automatically look to your mind to tell you what you are experiencing and what your response should be? What are you doing to build a relationship with your feelings and your body?

WHAT DO I DESIRE?

As a people pleaser and perfectionist, I had not the slightest idea of what I desired beyond what would please other people or would not rock the boat and attract unwanted attention. My behaviors did win me approval and praise, which, of course, everyone craves to some extent. It became self-reinforcing—I understood that if I behaved a certain way and accomplished certain things, then I would get approval and, with that, a sense of love and safety. If I did things differently, I would lose everything.

I wanted to say no to weekend practices because I knew that was what my body needed most, but I pushed through anyway because my coach expected it. I wanted to say no to traveling the world to competitions largely on my own, when what I desired most was companionship and support. I wanted to stand up for myself when my coach cut my scholarship funding, but instead I worked harder to prove that I deserved better. I stayed quiet or played along when men made inappropriate advances, when all I wanted to say was "How dare you" or "Fuck off." I wanted to allow myself to explore my sexuality more freely, but feared being used and judged. I wanted to admit that I was in over my head at times, but didn't want to disappoint people who expected me to have it all together.

This conditioned behavior isn't necessarily a logical thought process; rather, it's something that we adjust to and learn as we move through our early-childhood experiences. We have been trained and conditioned to not trust our desires—we are taught not to want too much, not to aspire too much, not to appear greedy or demanding. Our desires, we are warned, will lead us down a sinful path. We might also fear being disappointed if we follow what our hearts truly desire; we fear that we might get burned. And we certainly didn't learn how to attend to our desires.

But as we move into adulthood and learn to make our own decisions, there comes a point when we can continue to blindly seek the approval of and fit in to the status quo—our parents, our company, our society, our religion—or we can try to figure out what we each desire from this lifetime and follow our heart, our gut, our pussy, and our intuition. This is a choice and, I believe, a responsibility—to be skeptical and to question our lives and the world around us.

That's not to say that the answer we arrive at is always going to depart from the status quo, or that it has to be so black and white. What's important is the process of inquiring, being curious and skeptical, going inward. A desire-led life can very well mean that, after introspection, you determine that closely following religious doctrine is your calling in this life-time, that it lights you up, and that you will follow this path regardless of what others may expect from you.

Before my Saturn return, I didn't think to consider my needs and desires and whether my behaviors were actually going toward meeting them. But once I was no longer singu-larly focused on pleasing others and living up to societal ex-pectations and standards, I was presented with a gaping hole. Of course, I desired to have my basic needs met and to feel happy, safe, and loved. But I truly didn't know what this meant in the real world, what my heart and body desired in a prac-tical sense, in my lived experience. I didn't know what feel-ing happy, safe, and loved could look like for me—rather than what others told me it was.

I started to follow the bread crumbs and listen closely. I decided to pursue my psychic gifts, even though I knew peo-ple would judge me for it, because my desire to peer behind the veil and connect with Spirit was too great not to. Coming out of the spiritual closet brought me one step closer to my authentic self and led me to my coven. When the urge pre-sented itself, I dared to explore my sexual desires freely and casually, letting go of the restrictions of the "good girl" image and fully immersing myself in the taboo. Embracing my sex-uality, in self-pleasure practice and with a partner, has made me feel more whole. I could lay down the shame I carried and take back a piece of me that society so badly wants to control.

I decided to start a long-distance relationship during COVID, when all the odds were stacked against us. I chose to meet my partner in Tulum because I had a great desire to explore our potential. I allowed this desire to guide me to a beautiful relationship that logic had already written off as impossible.

Eventually, I discovered pleasure for myself. I learned to tap into my sensuality, to not only have a fulfilling sex life but also find pleasure in the process of living life. I learned that living from my true power means allowing my creativity to flow and my desire to lead the way.

Part of being able to access our desires is to understand the difference between needs, wants, and desires. Survival requires meeting our basic needs, while wanting something isn't as essential (and therefore sometimes comes with judgment or shame). We *need* enough protein, carbohydrates, fiber, and nutrients to survive; we *want* an organic green salad with dried cranberries, candied walnuts, and fresh goat cheese, with a side of sourdough straight out of the oven and slathered with butter.

Desires, meanwhile, are our strongest emotions and imply a potent intention. A yearning, a longing, a craving, an impulse drawing us to what we truly want.

Desires aren't sinful, selfish, or too much; ignoring our desires or punishing ourselves for them dims our light and extinguishes our fire. Mama Gena, author of *Pussy: A Reclamation*, describes desire as the direct interface between us and that which is greater than us: the Divine. Our desires are visions that lead to creation—and we as witches create from our womb space, our sensuality, our passion. Our desires connect us to our life-force energy as it moves through our bodies, as we enjoy and savor.

Living a desire-led life means trusting your desires as you trust your intuition. It means bringing awareness to what you desire and then taking actions that align. Desire and intuition aren't necessarily pointing us to a particular outcome but rather guiding us along a path of our highest purpose, the least resistance, and the most joy. Focusing our attention on what we truly desire, rather than on what we think we should want, is what creates the space for our desires to manifest.

If we can desire something, if we can visualize and feel the desire come to life, then we have already energetically created it. We are our own creators, and we have the power to create our own safety, happiness, and love. We can cocreate a beautiful life within our external environment.

I am convinced that we can all take a conscious step forward in our healing by acknowledging *who we are, what we feel, and what we desire.* All of this is already inside us, and that's our guide, our conscious healing elixir, to living a more attuned, embodied, and delicious life. A life lived as a W.I.T.C.H.

YOUR LEGACY, YOUR MANIFESTO

When you think about your moment of transition, what is it that *you* want to leave behind? A nice house and a hefty inheritance? Well, sure. We all want to take care of the people we love. But is that what will define your human experience, what you want to be remembered for?

This precious life can easily get away from us while we try to keep up with our daily obligations, spinning and spinning on the hamster wheel. It is up to us to redefine success from the constant hustle to living a more conscious life and aligning our actions with our purpose and desire. Living in harmony and in the flow of the subtle universal energies will make hard work not seem so hard because we aren't working against the natural flow, timing, and order of things.

If we define success as living up to our full potential and growing in life, then success is found in the process of living, in how we choose to show up for ourselves and others, and in how deeply we love, how much we are willing to face and heal, and how deeply we feel pleasure. It's the means, not the end; the work, not the outcome. While having a goal is necessary and affirming, reaching it simply isn't guaranteed. What is guaranteed, or, rather, what you can control, is how much and what kind of effort you put in.

I used to live by the Olympic motto, created in 1894 by Pierre de Coubertin—*"Citius, Altius, Fortius"* (Faster, Higher, Stronger)—for most of my life. Somehow, I completely missed the larger picture and forgot the Olympic creed.

> *The most important thing in life is not the triumph, but the fight; the essential thing is not to have won, but to have fought well.*

Today, I would replace *fight* with *journey* and *fought* with *lived*:

> *The most important thing in life is not the triumph, but the journey; the essential thing is not to have won, but to have lived well.*

I haven't mastered fully living in the present, always checking in with my intuition first, never being triggered by my core wounds, always letting my desires lead me, and never getting caught up in the hustle. And I never will, but I will keep inching closer. I will notice faster when I have fallen off track, reverted to old patterns and behaviors, and I will have tools, practices, and a coven to pick me up when I need a little extra help.

During the process of writing this book, the months and years of reflecting and processing, it was important for me to get clear on what it is that I actually want from life—at this moment in my journey, with what I know today. I decided to write a manifesto—to be that reminder of what "living well" means to me.

A personal manifesto is a statement describing values, principles, ideals, and intentions by which to live your life; it can help us evaluate the gap between our current reality and those principles or ideals, challenge assumptions and perspectives, and provoke change or recalibration of our behaviors to be in alignment with our values.

This is not a one-and-done exercise, and it isn't about getting it perfect; we actually want to review and reevaluate our manifesto on a regular basis. Life is fluid, and as we grow, encountering new experiences and challenges, our manifesto should reflect that as well.

MY MANIFESTO FOR A LIFE LIVED WELL

I follow the path of most joy in pursuit of my life's true purpose. Currently, I want to use more of my imagination and internal vision to break past the limits of my mind. Less worry, more inspiration, hope, and ease.

I have access to endless wisdom within. I trust that my wisdom and intuition guide me to my truth and won't let me lose sight of what truly matters: to love and be loved, to see and be seen, to hear and be heard, to know and be known, to be alive.

I know that I am always being guided. All I need to do is get out of my own way.

I vow to never stop growing emotionally, intellectually, and spiritually. I allow space to ponder and explore life's mysteries.

I vow to stay humble, to surrender, and to ask Spirit to "show me a better way" when I can't see past the limits of my human existence.

I vow to never put the needs and wants of others over

my own, unless it is my child who cannot meet his/her own needs yet.

Living a desire-led and pleasure-filled life is my birthright. I don't have to do or be anything to deserve this.

I know that I am a better and happier person when I commit to daily devotional, spiritual, and self-care practices.

I make a positive impact on the lives of those around me, be it with simple words of kindness, wisdom, or inspiration; by being generous with my time, resources, and my presence; by practicing forgiveness; by sharing compassion and love; by standing up for injustice; by living my truth.

I honor my body as the magical vessel it is. I treat my body with love, kindness, and respect. I take care of my body with proper nutrition and movement. I rest and recharge without guilt.

I vow to get closer to my true self, to peel back layer by layer, and to love all parts of me without judgment. I dare to show up and to allow myself to be seen fully.

I want to feel it all without the urge to change the experience. I allow my feelings to teach me.

I vow to walk through life with an open heart and with ease. I let my truth and my pleasure lead the way to true freedom. I am a free spirit.

I believe in a mind-body-spirit connection, and I will continuously work to balance my mind, my heart, and my pussy.

I vow to share my inner wisdom and wisdom from Spirit with the collective for the greatest good of all. I am a clear and honest channel.

I surrender to the things I cannot change, I welcome change with courage, and I trust my inner wisdom to help me be discerning.

I remember life is a gift, something to be honored, maintained, and enjoyed. It is not to be wasted.

REFLECTION

WHO AM I?
STEP 1:

Write out all the titles and roles that you have ever subscribed to or that have been assigned to you. You can come back to this exercise as often as you like, so there is no doing this right or wrong. Don't overthink it; just let it flow.

STEP 2:

Go through the list one by one and write down the answers to the following questions:

- Why do I subscribe to this title?
- Do I just accept it without questioning it?
- Do I define myself by using this title?
- What does it actually mean to me? Do I derive my personal value from it?
- Do I subscribe to it because it gives me societal status or because it is something I worked hard for?

STEP 3:

Go through this list and remove what no longer serves you or that which you have outgrown.

- How does it feel? How is your nervous system reacting to no longer identifying with this title?

STEP 4:

Add new descriptors that are more aligned with who you are today and the vision you have for yourself.

- What parts of me are not represented on this list?
- What are the parts I keep hidden because they might be "weird," "too much," or "unacceptable"?
- How does it feel to acknowledge these parts of myself?

STEP 5:

Now write a short paragraph to answer: *Who am I?* How do you feel and think about yourself when there is nobody to judge you? Keep refining as you grow and learn to embrace more aspects of yourself.

WHAT DO I FEEL?

- Can you identify what it is that you are feeling right now? Can you name the feeling? Where in your body does this feeling manifest and how? How does this feeling want to be expressed?
- What are the feelings that have been manifesting a lot lately? What is causing these feelings?
- In what ways could I honor my emotions without judgment? (Hint: What are you not honoring about yourself?)
- What are the feelings I want to call into my life more? What is stopping me from feeling these feelings?

WHAT DO I DESIRE?

- How much does your life turn you on?
- How much pleasure do you experience in everyday activities?
- Where in your life are you resisting pleasure? How are you restricting yourself?
- Write a desire list and describe your desires, big and small, with as much juicy detail as possible. Revisit this list often to cocreate your heart's desires.

TRY THIS: WRITE YOUR OWN MANIFESTO

Write a manifesto declaring what you want your legacy to be, and use it as a reminder when choosing how you want to live this life. There is no right or perfect way to do this, and you can be as creative with it as you please. Below are some ideas that helped me create my own.

STEP 1:

Get inspired and take notes. It is always easier to start with something rather than a blank sheet of paper.

- You can google "personal manifestos" and see what others have written to get inspired.
- If you've taken personality tests, read the results and see what stands out and resonates.
- Look at your astrological birth chart or your Gene Keys chart (or any other tools and methods you use) for additional insights into your life's purpose, challenges, and gifts.

- Look at lists of values and choose the ones that feel most authentic to you. Brené Brown has a great list of values on her website.
- Ask a few loved ones what they believe you stand for and see how their answers resonate.

STEP 2:

Create positive and affirmative statements that speak to you.

- Search for quotes and affirmations around a particular belief, intention, or value. You can use these verbatim, if they ring true for you and make you feel something.
- Fill in the blanks for the following:

I believe . . .

I vow . . .

I want to . . .

I desire to . . .

I aspire to . . .

I know my truth to be . . .

STEP 3:

Use words that feel good to you, that inspire and motivate you. Avoid words like "try"—be affirmative.

STEP 4:

Write your manifesto.

- You can write this in the form of a letter to your-self, a document, a bulleted list, or visual info-graphic or vision board.
- Keep it short and manageable so it doesn't start to feel overwhelming. Remember you can add and subtract as you please.

STEP 5:

Use it to live more mindfully. Incorporate it into your daily spiritual practice by reading it to yourself while drinking your morning coffee or tea. Remind yourself of your core values and your truth when you are faced with a difficult decision. Hang it somewhere you can be reminded of it.

STEP 6:

Revisit and revise regularly so it reflects where you are in your life.

AFTERWORD

We redefine our personal power by becoming Women in Total Conscious Healing. We find empowerment by embracing all parts of ourselves, the dark and the light; by becoming deeply sensual, intuitive, courageous women from the insight out; and by breaking the chains of labels and expectations. Living life unapologetically means allowing life to flow and be birthed through us, fully embodying our desires, and letting our senses guide us. There simply is no greater form of sovereignty and independence than trusting our own wisdom and our own bodies. If we acknowledge and fearlessly express our truth and embrace our inner feminine power, then we can pave a new road for ourselves and for future generations.

Spiritual awakening is not for the faint of heart. My hope is that in having read this book, you are one step closer to finding the courage to explore what is possible in your life and to feel empowered to make it a reality. We don't have to wait for a transformation or awakening; we can start right here, right now, one step at a time.

ACKNOWLEDGMENTS

I was guided to write this book as part of my own healing journey, but I couldn't have created it on my own. I want to give thanks and appreciation to all those who helped bring this vision to life. I apologize in advance if I've forgotten anyone.

Thanks to my spirit team, my loved ones, my guides, and my higher self for putting this idea in my heart and for guiding me to keep going when I wanted to give up.

Thanks to my family: Mom, Dad, Jason, and Keira, for all they have given me in this lifetime and for being the family I chose.

Thanks to all the gorgeous souls in my coven who held the vision for this book and who always believed in me: Matthias, Vicki, Renee, Katja, Becky, Andrea, Julie, Jason.

Thanks to all my teachers, mentors, healers, intuitives, and shamans who have taught me so much and who have had a tremendous impact on my healing journey: Janet Hariton, Stephen Robinson, Melissa Lee, Alexandra Roxo, Eduardo Placer, Christine Paradis, Wetsajoé, and the lovely spiritual communities at the Spiritualist Church of NYC, the Holistic Studies Institute, the Arthur Findlay College, and the Open Doorway.

Thanks to those who helped me navigate the book-writing and publishing process: Richelle Fredson, Anna Katz, and the team at Girl Friday Productions.

Thanks to all those souls who touched my life in one way or another, who agreed to be a part of my earth curriculum.

Thanks to you, dear reader, for taking the time to read this book and for being on this spiritual journey with me. I am honored that you have allowed me to be a part of your journey of self-discovery.

BIBLIOGRAPHY

Abbott, Karen. "The Fox Sisters and the Rap on Spiritualism." *Smithsonian*, October 30, 2012. https://www.smithsonianmag.com/history/the-E-sisters-and-the-rap-on-spiritualism-99663697/.

"About IFS." Foundation for Self Leadership. Updated 2022. https://www.foundationifs.org/about/about-ifs#:~:text=IFS%2C%20founded%20in%20the%20early,psychotherapy%20modality%20%26%20a%20mental%20paradigm.

Bernstein, Gabby. "My SuperSoul Sessions Talk: The 5 Steps to Spiritual Surrender." *GabbyBernstein.com* (blog), July 26, 2018. https://gabbybernstein.com/new-blog-super-soul-sessions-talk-5-steps-spiritual-surrender/.

Brown, Brené. "Dare to Lead: List of Values." https://brenebrown.com/resources/dare-to-lead-list-of-values/.

Choquette, Sonia. *Tune In: Let Your Intuition Guide You to Fulfillment and Flow.* United States: Hay House Inc., 2013.

Cleghorn, Elinor. *Unwell Women: Misdiagnosis and Myth in a Man-Made World.* New York: Dutton, 2021.

Comas-Díaz, Lillian, and Marcella Bakur Weiner. "Sisters of the Heart: How Women's Friendships Heal." *Women & Therapy* 36 (2013).

Dass, Ram. *Ram Dass, Going Home.* 2018; Netflix. https://www.netflix.com/title/80209895.

Estés, Clarissa Pinkola. *Women Who Run with the Wolves: Myths and Stories of the Wild Woman Archetype*. New York: Ballantine Books, 1996.

Fossella, Tina, and John Welwood. "Human Nature, Buddha Nature: An Interview with John Welwood." *Tricycle: The Buddhist Review* 20, no. 3 (Spring 2011).

French, Michael. *Why Men Fall Out of Love: What Every Woman Needs to Understand*. New York: Ballantine Books, 2007.

Gibson, Lindsay C. *Adult Children of Emotionally Immature Parents: How to Heal from Distant, Rejecting, or Self-Involved Parents*. Oakland, CA: New Harbinger Publications, 2015.

Hundley, Jessica, ed. *Witchcraft: The Library of Esoterica*. Cologne: Taschen, 2021.

Kierkegaard, Søren. *Kierkegaard's Journals and Notebooks, vol. 11, part 1: Loose Papers, 1830–1843*. Princeton, NJ: Princeton University Press, 2019.

National Geographic Society. "The Development of Agriculture." *National Geographic*, https://education.nationalgeographic.org/resource/development-agriculture.

Noble, Vicki. *Shakti Woman: Feeling Our Fire, Healing Our World: The New Female Shamanism*. San Francisco: HarperSanFrancisco, 1991.

"Our Organization." National Spiritualist Association of Churches, https://nsac.org/who-we-are/our-organization/.

Oxford Dictionary of Phrase and Fable. 2nd ed. New York: Oxford University Press, 2006.

"Quotable Quotes." Reader's Digest Association, January 1957.

Pueblo, Yung. *Clarity &Connection*. Andrews McMeel Publishing, 2021.

Rapkin, Brett, dir. *The Weight of Gold*. Aired 2020, on HBO.

"Richard Schwartz." Good Therapy. Updated 2022. https://www
.goodtherapy.org/famous-psychologists/richard
-schwartz.html#:~:text=Richard%20Schwartz%20is%20
a%20contemporary,Model%20(IFS)%20of%20therapy.

Roxo, Alexandra. *F*ck Like a Goddess: Heal Yourself. Reclaim
Your Voice. Stand in Your Power.* Boulder: Sounds True,
July 2020.

Rumi, Jalal al-Din. *The Essential Rumi.* San Francisco:
HarperOne, 2004.

Schucman, Helen, and Bill Thetford. *A Course in Miracles:
Combined Volume.* 3rd ed. Mill Valley, CA: Foundation for
Inner Peace, 1975.

Silver, Tosha. *It's Not Your Money: How to Live Fully from
Divine Abundance.* 1st ed. Carlsbad, CA: Hay House, Inc.,
2019.

Stone, Merlin. *When God Was a Woman.* Boston: Mariner
Books, 1978.

Swan, Teal. "Quote: Condemn Sexuality." https://tealswan
.com/quotes/condemn-sexuality-r782/.

"ThetaHealing." *ThetaHealing* (blog). https://www.thetahealing
.com/blog/thetahealing/.

Thomashauer, Regena. *Pussy: A Reclamation.* Carlsbad, CA:
Hay House, Inc., 2016.

Wallis, Christopher. "The Real Story on the Chakras." *Hareesh,*
February 5, 2016. https://hareesh.org/blog/2016/2/5/the
-real-story-on-the-chakras.

Wineland, John. "The Dance of the Masculine & Feminine."
Online master class given February 23, 2022. https://www
.johnwineland.com/masterclass-the-dance-of-masculine
-and-feminine.

Wong, Brittany. "What Is Toxic Productivity? Here's How to
Spot the Damaging Behavior." *HuffPost,* April 5, 2021.
https://www.huffpost.com/entry/toxic-productivity
-work_l_606655e7c5b6aa24bc60a566.

ABOUT THE AUTHOR

Siobhan Claire is a multipassionate intuitive. As an Olympic athlete, corporate executive, intuitive consultant, psychic medium, ordained minister, writer, and entrepreneur, she is proof that you do not have to fit the mold. In her teachings, Siobhan draws upon her life experiences, her spiritual training and ever-evolving spiritual path, and metaphysical principles, as well as techniques that have made her successful as an athlete and professional.

In her spare time, Siobhan loves to explore the world, stay fit, try new restaurants, enjoy time outdoors, dance, make love, learn, write, expand her spiritual gifts, and spend as much time as possible with her coven and her family.

Born in Germany to Irish and Scottish parents, Siobhan moved to the United States in 2004 for college. Today she lives in New York City with her partner.

For more information on Siobhan's work, visit www .siobhanclaire.com.

CPSIA information can be obtained
at www.ICGtesting.com
Printed in the USA
BVHW032007150223
658591BV00004B/239